March 2018

To Michael Bowman

God bless you,

Rhonda J. Goff

ROAD TRIP: JESUS, JEREMY *and* ME

Rhonda J. Goff

WESTBOW
PRESS®
A DIVISION OF THOMAS NELSON
& ZONDERVAN

Copyright © 2017 Rhonda J. Goff.

All rights reserved. No part of this book may be used or reproduced by any means, graphic, electronic, or mechanical, including photocopying, recording, taping or by any information storage retrieval system without the written permission of the author except in the case of brief quotations embodied in critical articles and reviews.

THE HOLY BIBLE, NEW INTERNATIONAL VERSION®, NIV® Copyright © 1973, 1978, 1984, 2011 by Biblica, Inc.® Used by permission. All rights reserved worldwide.

WestBow Press books may be ordered through booksellers or by contacting:

WestBow Press
A Division of Thomas Nelson & Zondervan
1663 Liberty Drive
Bloomington, IN 47403
www.westbowpress.com
1 (866) 928-1240

The views expressed in this work are solely those of the author and do not necessarily reflect the views of the publisher, and the publisher hereby disclaims any responsibility for them.

Any people depicted in stock imagery provided by Thinkstock are models,
and such images are being used for illustrative purposes only.
Certain stock imagery © Thinkstock.

ISBN: 978-1-5127-8863-1 (sc)
ISBN: 978-1-5127-8864-8 (hc)
ISBN: 978-1-5127-8862-4 (e)

Library of Congress Control Number: 2017908062

Print information available on the last page.

WestBow Press rev. date: 6/19/2017

This is a true story of the Holy Spirit in His work of
loving, comforting, teaching, and saving.
To God be the glory.

In memory of my son, Jeremy Shane Ockerman.
Born July 11, 1978
Died May 19, 1996

To Jeremy's grandparents:
Johnnie and Joyce Goff
and
Thurman and Connie Ockerman.

To my parents, Johnnie and Joyce Goff, who gave me a wonderful Christian home. They supported my Christian education and showed me how to build my Christian life on the rock foundation of Jesus Christ. They lived their lives in such a way that set the finest of examples. They lived what they believed. I thank them for it.

And to Billy's parents, Thurman and Connie Ockerman. They treated me like a daughter. They were not only my good in-laws; they were my friends. They were full of love, support, and encouragement until their days were over on this earth and they passed on to their eternal homes in heaven. I thank them for it.

Contents

Part I Introduction

1. Mystery 1
2. Godly Encouragement and Acknowledgments 6
3. Connection 11
4. Faith 14

Part II Life Changed

5. Jeremy and Dustin 27
6. Eternity 35
7. Death Is the Bridge 39
8. My Grief 42

Part III Between Heaven and Earth

9. The Sword of Death 47
10. The Goodbye Hug 51
11. The Golden Rule 55
12. Love beyond Measure 61
13. God's Baby Book 67
14. Psalm 139 71
15. God Is Still in Control 74

Part IV From Heaven to Earth

16 It's Like the Wind 84
17 Amazing Grace 94
18 Sweet Amanda 99
19 Our Sweet Jeremy 102
20 The Letter and Jeremy's Poem 105
21 Blessed Assurance 107

Part V Drowning in Sorrow

22 Graduation 113
23 The Lights Go Out 115
24 My Dream 121
25 My Heart Shatters 124
26 Why? 127
27 Side Streets and Detours 131
28 Guilt 137
29 The Newspaper 140
30 Driven to the Cemetery 146
31 Safe from the Evil 150
32 Dear Jeremy 159
33 Like a Rock 164

Part VI Presence on Earth and in Heaven

34 Presence 169
35 Church 176
36 A Family Visitor 183
37 My Visit from Mary 187
38 Jesus 192
39 Jesus Came 196

Part VII Life Goes On

40 The Kodak Moment 207
41 Working at School 209
42 Grieving Parents 212
43 Madelyn 214
44 Out of the Blue 218

Part VIII Home

45 One God 227
46 The Holy Bible 232
47 I'll See You at Church in the Morning! 235
48 Jesus Is Coming Back 237
49 Home 242

Author's Notes 247

Part I

INTRODUCTION

MYSTERY

God says there *is* life after physical death. I don't know about you, but I'm not going to argue with Him about that. In fact, I like that idea very much. Actually, I love that idea. I ask myself, "Why would I want to believe otherwise?"

Of course I answer myself: "I don't. No way do I want to believe otherwise."

I believe in God, so I believe that what He says is true. It's not just a wonderful idea; it is a fact. Our loved ones seem dead to us because we can no longer see, touch, feel, or hear them. They are not here physically with us, but they are not dead. They are still alive. They are *invisible*. They have left this physical world and have entered into the heavenly realm of peace, joy, and bliss. They are happy. This spiritual world they have entered is beyond description, beyond anything that we as humans can ever comprehend. It is hard to imagine something that I can't even comprehend. It sounds absolutely thrilling, and I'm 100 percent sure it is.

It is only the physical part of us that dies. We know that these bodies of ours will die someday. Physical death is ahead for every one of us. This physical part of us, this body we see, is not made to last forever. It is a temporary body. It seems like a bummer because we are tied to the earth, and we hate to give it up, *and* we hate to give our loved ones up. It is natural for us to feel this way. God made us to want to enjoy life here on earth and love each other and not want to be separated.

In reality, though, He has something better in mind for our future. It is a blessing that we don't have to continue to live forever in old, weak, sick bodies that will never get any better. I'm looking older day by day, getting older and feeling older in my body, but one of these days, that's going to change, and my soul and spirit, which I do not see with these physical eyes of mine, will fly away to everlasting life to live with God forever. Wow, I don't know about you, but I'm kind of excited about that flying away part too (Psalms 90:10).

Our souls and spirits are who we are. It is the Word of God that can penetrate to divide soul and spirit. It is sharper than any double-edged sword (Hebrews 4:12). I will be referring to soul/spirit as one unit. They work together. My soul/spirit lives in my physical body. I don't understand, but I believe; therefore, I *know*. It is a knowing in my spirit, in the deepest recesses of my eternal soul. I will live forever. My body is temporary and will die, but I am not temporary. Yay—I love that! That information is energizing, encouraging, and exciting. What a thought to dwell on. It makes me want to cheerlead with pompoms! It makes me want to shoot baskets, run around the bases, race to the finish line, sing, dance, high-five! I will live forever. *You* will live forever. Our separation is only *temporary*.

In 2 Corinthians 5:7, it says as Christians, we walk by faith, not by what we see. Faith is better than sight anyway. Faith is a drink of water and food to our souls. Yes, our souls have to be fed too. Faith gives strength, joy, and peace to life. Faith is eternal. It is a *knowing* inside that we carry around with us no matter where we go, no matter what we see or don't see. No matter what happens or doesn't happen, we have our faith inside of us. Thank God that He has revealed faith to us. He has given us a lifeline that is an invisible substance that keeps us afloat in this world. It keeps us linked to heaven … to that world we cannot physically see. We sure know it's there all the same even though we can't see it. And we *need* to know it's there. God knows we need to know it's there, and He has given us a way to know. He extends His hands out, offering faith to us.

All is well!

Faith is definitely a mystery.

It is a miracle and a blessing.

And it is a gift!

My faith in God allows me to believe; it gives me spiritual strength to accept the fact that I don't understand the mysteries, and that's okay.

I don't have to understand to believe.

Actually, that is backward.

Let's get it in the right order.

I must *believe* in order to understand.

Wait, there's more!

My biggest understanding is the fact that I don't have to understand. Isn't that amazing and wonderful? What a relief! The pressure is off!

It's just like when my children were small, and they didn't understand everything I did for them in discipline and love. How could they understand? They weren't equipped yet to understand. They had to rely on trust. Neither am I equipped to understand everything about my heavenly Father. Therefore, trusting Him is what I do.

God revealed mysteries to me from the spiritual world that is all around us. He gave *spiritual events* that were confirmations of His great love. Even though they were not concrete, they were very real, and each one was based upon truth. He poured mercy all over me.

"Blessed are those who mourn, for they will be comforted" (Matthew 5:4 NIV).

Mourning is horrible. It is agony. Mourning is devastatingly painful. Mourning is ugly. Mourning and grieving are parts of this life we have to deal with. We have to go through it. None of us get by without it, unless we die before we experience it.

Jesus blesses those of us who are mourning, those of us who are heartbroken, those of us who have crushed spirits, those of us who are wounded and bleeding, no matter the reason. He tells us that we will be comforted. Those are not just pretty words. They are living truth. Jesus said these words, and He meant them. Jesus never said anything He didn't mean. I was blessed—made joyous—throughout my mourning. God's mercy made the mourning bearable. It was all a *mystery*.

God taught me about forever. Forever is a continuous, miraculous event that was hard for me to fathom. Part of that was the fact that I didn't think about including it in my daily life. I thought forever was something far off when this life is over. This is not truth. The truth is—forever has already started! It is already a part of me. To include this in my daily life is powerful. It really is. It changes everything about the way I think about living. I am going to live *forever*. My life has no end, and I know my life will just get better and better. Oh, yes, pain is of this world and will be on and off down here on earth, but it is only temporary. I will be going home soon, and in the meantime, I want to experience as much of this temporary earthly trip as I can. Every minute counts and is linked in a beautiful continuation that will go on and on forever! It is only my physical body that will die. I will keep living. Knowing these things in my mind enhances my thinking and my senses, chasing away darkness that comes. I wish these things wouldn't come, but they do. What can I say? I accept it. Part of life is what it is. I always have hope that things will pass, that things will get better, and they will—and they do. It is a mystery how God can take all my experiences and make them work for my good.

This brings my forever into the present moment. It helps keep this life in perspective, renews my spirit, gives me energy, and strengthens my faith. I know that anything is possible every day with God in my life (Matthew 19:26). It helps me remember that God is in control. Praise His holy name!

Once life has begun, it is automatically forever. Eternity is in us, and it goes with us when our physical bodies die. We will live forever. There are two choices we have about eternal life. One is to live in eternal bliss with our Father God through His Son Jesus Christ. The other is to not choose God, not accept His Son, and not accept His mercy and grace. I choose God and His Son. I choose light, love, and bliss. I don't want it any other way.

I will be weaving the Holy Bible in with my true story. I will be talking about some of the people in the Bible who have helped me in my journey to survive. Abraham, Job, Nicodemus, David, Peter, Paul, James, and Mary are a few of the people who gave me strength while I traveled the road of grief. These people are alive. They are going to live forever. The Bible is *alive* (Hebrews 4:12). It is the Word of God, and the Word of God is the Author and Giver of a life that is *forever*. It is a *mystery*. The Living God is *mysterious*. Praise His holy name! My most precious companion traveling with me on my road of grief was my loving Savior, Jesus Christ our Lord. He never left me. Taking this road trip was not my idea. But it happened. I did not travel alone. Jesus, Jeremy, and I traveled it together. Jesus taught me so much. The Holy Trinity never left me.

We will all live together forever. I want to wake up every morning praising God and with the thought that we will live forever with God. What a way to start the day! My head is in the sky, my heart is set on heaven, and my soul is longing for home. It is the greatest of all futures. We have so much to look forward to.

GODLY ENCOURAGEMENT AND ACKNOWLEDGMENTS

Whenever I would tell my family and friends what I've experienced, people would say to me, "You should write a book."

I felt the same thing too. Each one of you who has said that to me confirmed what I was feeling. Those of you who have said it have no idea how your precious words have echoed at me down through the years. They became embedded in my heart, and they kept coming to my mind. That's because words are powerful. There is power in our thoughts. There is power in written words. There is power in spoken words. Words are powerful, living things.

It was with words that God created this world (Genesis 1:3 NIV)!

We find that God continued to create the world with words throughout the first chapter of the book of Genesis. You know what? He did not keep us wondering about it. We do not have to scratch our heads and wonder where in the world … did this world come from? Isn't that marvelous? It is the very first thing He tells us! He introduces Himself to us by telling us that in the beginning He created everything. He tells us right off the bat what He did with the very first verse of His Book, and He tells us how He did it in the following verses. Do we understand such a thing with our minds only? Of course not. How could we? However, that's okay. It's not an understanding of humankind's mind. He made another way for us to understand it. He made it exciting. We have to search for it. If we search for it in the right place, it's easy to find. The right place is in our hearts and in the depths of our souls. He put it in us. That is the first step. We must yearn for answers. He loves for us to search for answers about Him and His ways. He loves for us to ask, seek, and knock. He will bring it right to us. He has laid it all out in His Book, and through His Holy Spirit, He teaches us. Wow! Oh, thank You, God!

God has also given this gift of "creating with words" to us ... yes, to *us*. We are like our Father. That just makes me smile! We are His children, made in His image (Genesis 1:27). Who are we like? We are like *Him*. He gave us free choice on how we want to use our own words. He gave us free choice on what we want to create with them. We are made like Him.

We know in our hearts that words have the power to create or destroy, make us or break us. Words come out of us in many ways, and sometimes—oh, yes—sometimes we forget we have this power. However, this power is there all the same whether we are mindful of it or not. It does its work no matter what we're saying. It is important to remember this power that we have, but it is easy to forget it!

Words in the Bible have great Holy Spirit-inspired power. The Bible is the Word of God. Isn't that fascinating? I think it is. They are His words. He can talk to us. He *wants* to talk to us. He has made it available. If we want to unlock the power of His words to us, there is one ingredient we must have. That ingredient is faith. We have to believe He wants to talk to us and that the Bible is His Word. It doesn't have to be a great, huge lump of faith either. He can use it even if it is as small as a little, tiny mustard seed (Luke 17:6). That is very small, but that's okay. It's a start, and seeds grow into great things when they are watered and taken care of.

I am a visual person. I like to create pictures in my mind to help me remember things and bond with them. I like to say that my faith (no matter what size it is) has many keys (endless keys) that unlock heavenly treasures in the Bible. I visualize a big key ring with the word *faith* etched into some wood that is hanging from the key chain. Then I see the faith keys that hang from this key ring that can unlock treasure after treasure. Oh, how rich I am! I can be wealthy with these keys of faith. God has given me free choice whether or not I use these keys. Oh, yes, He has, and I am amazed at that too. Freedom, freedom, freedom! He knows we love freedom. He knows we love choices. I am the keeper of the keys (that's just the way He wants it), and I can personally unlock treasures He has for me and use them in my life. I like to carry my faith keys with me everywhere I go. I can name a key whatever I want to and anytime I want to, according to the need in my life, and He will meet me there. Can that be beat? No way!

These treasures I unlock are the verses in the Bible that are filled to the brim with His rich words (yes, His words) that can give me exactly what I need when I need it. I can go to my heavenly Father about anything and everything. Isn't that fantastic? It's like constantly searching for new treasures and finding them. I have always liked those TV shows and movies where people are searching for secret treasures. I just feel like I am right there with them in the search, and it is exciting and thrilling.

God has given me a way to search for His treasures anytime I want to—and to find them. God the Creator knows me, knows what I personally need, and delivers it to me through His words. Oh, what wonderful words! These heavenly treasures are alive just like we are.

Some of the things He tells us in these heavenly treasures are ways we are to treat each other since we are His children. He is very concerned about that, you know. We understand His concern because we want our children to treat each other well too. The opposite is true also. We do not want our children to take bad treatment from another. That is not right or good. We are made like our Father. We are adopted brothers and sisters to His one and only begotten Son. This makes us one big family. Oh, we don't ever have to be lonely because we have family everywhere. He wants us to be one unit, and He's very concerned about how we treat each other. We won't always get it right because it is a learning, growing experience that lasts a lifetime. We work on it with God's help. When we put our faith in these verses that our heavenly Father has freely given to us, they start working inside of us so we will become more like our brother Jesus. Here is one of those beautiful power-packed verses that I am talking about. This is one of those treasures that other people (and you know who you are) have unlocked and given to me.

"Therefore encourage one another and build each other up, just as in fact you are doing" (1 Thessalonians 5:11 NIV).

This is one of our instructions from our heavenly Father. Don't you just love it? We are supposed to be encouragers and builder-uppers. We are not to tear each other down. We are builders. He even encouraged the Thessalonians to keep doing it by telling them they were doing it already. He encouraged and praised them through Paul to keep up the good work.

We are always to continue in our efforts to encourage, and I thank the Lord God of creation for giving me such great encouragers. My spirit has been strengthened by such kind, loving, supportive words. I have received such beautiful words from my Christian brothers and sisters in Christ, and these special words have *lived* in me. I have hung on to these words whenever I have needed support. This wonderful support system that God has given me has been backed by the Word of God and is a holy gift. Holy gifts are the very best gifts we can give to each other! Encouragement is a holy gift from heaven. It is one of the finest gifts ever. Encouragement lifts the spirit. Holy gifts touch my soul and help my *soul (who I really am)* to live the life that is meant to be lived. Your loving encouragement and faith in me has been spiritual nourishment to all of who I am. Your wonderful support has helped to keep my mind, heart, and soul engaged in not forgetting my priorities. Just sitting here thinking of all you wonderful people of encouragement in my life gives me so much comfort and joy that I feel uplifted in my spirit in a mighty and powerful way. Oh … what … a … feeling! My spirit soars inside with thankfulness, love, and joy.

I am not going to name names, because there are too many, and I definitely don't want to leave anyone out. You know who you are. You will feel it in your soul—yes, you will—that I am thanking you personally, and I have been blessed by you. When you feel it deep inside you, don't quench it! That's the Holy Spirit confirming it. Smile, enjoy it, and be blessed by it!

You are scattered all across this county I live in and in other counties, other states, and one other country. Many of you I have known all my life, others for a few years, and others are new acquaintances. Some of you have even already passed over into heaven. Yes, you have, but I know you hear me, and I know that you are still cheering me on. Oh, how lovely! Oh, how sweet! All of you are my wonderful friends.

I'm not finished talking about it, because even though it has been all these years, I still have people ask me if I have my book finished yet! Isn't that something? Sometimes I'm just in awe that you remember. This tells me you still have faith in me to do it. Wow, oh, wow! Here we go again about the power of faith.

Faith in each other is power-packed too.

Your faith in me strengthens me and has strengthened me through the years, no matter what life was dealing me at the time. Your faith in me has been the other encouragement I have needed in order to never give up. You want me to write this book, and that is the finest support anyone could ever have. Your faith in me helps me to move the mountains that Satan throws in my way to stop me, even if I have to use a shovel to get it done.

Now, I know I have gone on and on about this, but I feel it strongly in my heart, mind, and spirit that I have to express it to the fullest. You are helpers in getting this book out to the world. I love you all. As we work together in unity with one heart and one mouth, we glorify the God and Father of our Lord Jesus Christ. You know who you are, God knows who you are, and I thank you from the bottom of my heart.

"May the God who gives endurance and encouragement give you a spirit of unity among yourselves as you follow Christ Jesus, so that with one heart and mouth you may glorify the God and Father of our Lord Jesus Christ" (Romans 15:5–6 NIV).

CONNECTION

It is early morning for me right now as I sit here typing with you on my mind. I am sitting in the living room on the couch, cup of coffee by my side, looking out of the front window. The sun has captured my attention. It just now peeked over the horizon. My eyes move to the stretch of trees in the far distance, and I take in all the rounded, rolling hills and the green, mowed meadows that surround those trees. This view is spectacular at all times of the day. I can see for miles and miles. I have to say though that this particular morning has an added beauty as the sun shines through a light smoky fog that is rolling in from the Chaplin River. I cannot see the river from here, because it lies behind everything in my view, but it is making its presence known by the rising fog. Oh, what a creation! The sun coming up, the dawn of a new day, the river and the air creating fog, the majesty of the moment….it is all so wonderful. I just have to stop and gasp at this breathtaking sight that God has created for us to live in, both His skies and His earth. I praise His holy name.

After I have soaked in all the magnificent wonder of the start of morning (and added my gratefulness for this good, steaming cup of coffee to top it off!), I look down at this laptop, and I feel God has set all green lights that say, "Go! Now is the time!"

My spirit absolutely soars as I feel this truth. Oh, what a grand feeling when my spirit soars within me! It is a feeling like no other, and it is fellowship with God. It comes from deep within. I feel connected to God, to myself, and to you. This is the way it is supposed to be. And in the order it is supposed to be. This is a secret within life itself that we are not born knowing. No, as little babies, we do not have a clue. It is in us, but we have to grow into it. It is an unfolding in our lives like a rose bud that grows into a full and beautiful rose. We grow. We learn as we let God teach us about Himself, about life, about this world and the world to come.

I feel this connection right now, so when I say I am ready to go forward, it is because I have wanted to share so many things with you for a long, long time. In fact, it has been years. I have had this book on bits and pieces of paper put away in a suitcase, then in a trunk, then handwritten in a notebook, then typed up and put in a binder as I wrote down my experiences, but I never had the power to put them together in completion. I referred to them as my quilt pieces ready to be made into a beautiful, colorful quilt that would be created to cover you with warm comfort and love. Sometimes I referred to them as precious jewels in my treasure chest just waiting to be strung together as a mighty fine necklace and gift to you.

I tried and tried to put it together sooner, but God had many things to teach me. I guess I'll tell you a little bit about that.

The very first thing He wanted to teach me was how to put Him first in my life, not the book or anything else. I thought I was putting Him first my whole life, but I wasn't. I just didn't know I wasn't. You see, most of my life, I was putting church first. Well, that sure was out of order. I was spending more time doing His work than spending personal, intimate time with Him. God is supposed to be first; I am supposed to fill myself with Him second, and then church flows out of that to do His work. The main thing was that I was trying. I wanted to put Him first, and He knew it. I had the desire. This also involved everything in my life, and it was a lot for me to learn. I'm telling you, it took a lot of hard knocks, a lot of sweet revelations, and a long time. But, that's okay. Better late than never, right? God does not give up on teaching. Of course, my spiritual makeover is an ongoing project and will be until my last dying breath. Through it all so far, this is one big whopping lesson I have learned: I have learned that God's timing is the only time in which to do anything for Him. It is not about me, and it's not about my time. It's not about what I want, but it's about His time and what He wants. He has the whole picture. I sure don't. If I work in my time without Him, I have left out my partnership with Him and also put myself before Him. Oh, no! That is so out of order.

It has taken time for Him to teach me this, and of course, I am still learning. He has had patience with me (that's because He loves me, which is the grandest thing!) while I have learned and continue to learn about Him and His ways. If you are holding this book in your hands, you will know without a shadow of a doubt it is in your hands because of God's timing ... not mine. It is in His timing that you are reading it for the benefit of your own personal life! Isn't it absolutely wonderful how God pulls it all together? It's kind of a jaw-dropping thing when I stop to think about it. God is all knowing and mysterious in His astonishing and glorious ways.

We are all united together in this big wonderful world even though we are all separate. Now that all this connection has been made with my putting God first, filling myself with Him, I am ready to do His will. I want to share with you what I consider to be a marvelous yet heartbreaking true story that came into my life many years ago. I want to tell you how the Holy Spirit came like the wind in many forms to comfort and restore me. Here we go. Walk down the roads of agony, despair, grief, love, joy, and peace that passed all understanding with Jesus, Jeremy, and me.

FAITH

I have to say that after all this time, when someone mentions that year 1996, I feel a spring inside me that cringes. It is because that year is way down deep in me. Oh, yes, it is. It is deep in my memory, deep down in my subconscious and conscious mind, deep in my heart, and it is burned deep into my everlasting soul. It will always be a part of me for as long as I live, and that will be for eternity. I will not have the pain, sorrow, and tears for eternity, because God will wipe all of that away forever, but I will carry the scars of it all just like Jesus carries His, and that's okay. My scars are mine. They are all a part of who I am. They are maps of where I have been while traveling on this journey called earthly life. They are a reminder of how God was always there no matter what I was going through and no matter what I had gotten myself into. He was always there to teach, guide, and instruct me. He was always there to forgive me. He was always there to comfort and restore me. He was always there to love me through all the maneuvering of living I did. No matter where I am, no matter what is going on in my life, God is always there with me. It also includes all the times it doesn't seem like He is there. The truth is that wherever I am, no matter what I am doing, no matter what I am thinking, no matter what is going on in my life, God is with me. There is another thing for certain too: He did not put the scars there. Life did. However, He was always there to help me overcome and heal the deep wounds I received, and now only the scars remain.

ROAD TRIP: JESUS, JEREMY AND ME

Even though I say I cringe every time someone mentions the year 1996, at the same, I am in awe of the mysteries that God Almighty revealed to me that year. Oh my goodness! What mysteries! God is mysterious. Oh, what a thrill to think about that. He is God. Now, it's not that He revealed facts about these mysteries. I don't have any details on how any of it happened, but in all honesty, I really don't need facts because God has given me faith, and through my faith, I know, I know, I know! I know in my mind, I know in my heart, and I know in my spirit that these mysteries were miracles, and I can rest assured that I don't have to understand it in my head. I don't have to know how any of it happened because miracles are simply not understood. They don't have to be. They just are!

Every time Jesus performed a miracle in the Bible, people were astonished, astounded, and amazed. Could they explain any of them with human reasoning? No!

Did they understand any of them with human reasoning? No!

When Jesus performed His first miracle of turning the water into wine at the wedding banquet, He revealed His glory, and it was at this moment that His disciples put their faith in Him (John 2:11). What a monumental moment! What a day! What a change took place in their lives when this happened!

His miracles were glory just as He is glory. The things that happened to me, miracles I call them, just *were*, kind of like the fact that I just *am*, and they were filled with glory. They were also filled with comfort and love.

How do I know they were real and not just my imaginings? I *know* because my brain had nothing to do with it! I *know* because they came when I did not expect them!

There is no other way to explain it! I know where they came from because of my faith in God Almighty. Faith is my key, and I've already mentioned this key to you. Oh what a glorious key! Faith is my key to accepting what happened to me in the same way that faith is my key in believing in God, believing in the Holy Bible, believing in God's Son Jesus Christ, and believing in the Holy Spirit. I cannot brush them off as anything but what they truly were! I know without a doubt that they were miracles coming from the comfort of the Holy Spirit's presence. Yes, they were.

My faith is the same faith that the disciples had when they put their faith in Jesus at that wedding banquet. It is the same faith that all of us have within our very own souls who proclaim that Jesus is the Christ, the Son of the Living God. Faith reveals the truth that says God is very much alive and still performs miracles, and it is faith that believes that truth! Oh, how marvelous!

So, if faith is the key, then what is this thing called faith? It is a beautiful thing to ponder such a glorious, wonderful thing as faith! The Lord loves for us to ponder His great gifts!

Hebrews 11:1 (NIV, my personal comments added):
"Now faith is being sure (absolutely, positively 100 percent sure)
(Sure of what?)
of what we hope for (Oh, wow!)
and certain of what we do not see." (No doubts!)

Did that say that faith is being sure of what we hope for even though we do not see it? Oh, how wonderful! What do we hope for in life? Does this faith have to do with everyday earthly life, minute by minute, even though we can't see it? Oh, yes! It has everything to do with everything in life. This includes everything that we do in life, from our first breath until our last breath. Faith is the gasoline for our spiritual engines whether we realize it or not. Faith is our constant fuel that keeps us going. Many times we don't even know we have it. However, we know when we don't have it. We can definitely see and feel those results. What happens when we lose faith in living? What happens when we feel we have no hope? We give up on living. Hope and faith are intertwined. Hope is expecting and looking for something good to happen. Faith is having trust in that hope. I have felt hopeless before, and it led to depression, unhappiness, turmoil, anxiety, and misery. I could definitely see those things in me, and so could other people. Hopelessness and having no faith are terrible enemies.

Hope and faith give life. They give life to our physical bodies, and they give life to the spirits of our souls.

God has given us free will in what we hope for! Right now, my hope is that many people read this book I am writing. I have faith in my hope. I cannot physically see you reading this book, but I have faith that you are.

The writer of Hebrews tells us more about this marvelous, wonderful gift of faith and how it affects our understanding of God Almighty.

Hebrews 11:3 (NIV):
"By faith we understand
that the universe was formed at God's command, (oh my!)
so that what is seen
was not made out of what was visible." (I look up at the sky in reverence and worship God who commanded it to be formed out of the invisible!)

Faith means we believe in the invisible. Invisible, invisible, invisible is here, there, and everywhere! We know there is more to life than just what we can see with our physical eyes and what we know with our other physical senses. It is by faith that we understand that God exists even though He is invisible to us, and it is by faith that we understand that the universe was made out of things that we can't see. The vastness of the universe is astounding to me, and then to think it was made out of something I can't even see is breathtaking, mind-boggling, and amazing. This thought really opens my eyes to the spiritual world.

Well, where does this understanding that he is talking about come from? How can I understand and believe all this without question?

This understanding comes from the *knowing* that God put in us when He created us! It goes all the way back to the creation.

Romans 1:20 (NIV):
"For since the creation of the world
God's invisible qualities—his eternal power and divine nature—
have been clearly seen, (Clearly seen? Really? How?)
being understood from (Understood from what?)
what has been made, (Oh my!)
so that men are without excuse."

There it is. God tells us all about it in His Word. Isn't He so good to explain it to us? This understanding is already within us. How did it get in us? He says He put it there. However, He gave us free will to find it if we want it. It is entirely up to us. It must be born in us and by each of us, and the way it is born is by believing in God even if we can't see Him! It is marvelously simple! Oh, how He wants us to see it! When we go outside and look at all of God's stunning creation (which is a never-ending pilgrimage, because there is so much to see in this world), when we really, really look at each other as His last and best of what He created (which would take more than an earthly lifetime because we are all so unique and wonderfully made), when we marvel at the miraculous birth of a baby (which still never ceases to amaze me. When our children were born, I thought, *How did we do that?* And you know what I mean!), when we see the rebirth of trees and flowers in the spring (which is a wonder to behold as nature gently unfolds), when we look at all these things that have life, God says we already know Him! He is in everything! The knowledge is already there within us, but if we refuse to admit all this wonder and glory and refuse to acknowledge it, then God says we have absolutely no excuse before Him on that great judgment day. That's because it is right before our eyes. We have to open our eyes!

We get to this "knowing" and this "understanding of the knowing" by believing. It is that simple! That is called faith. And when this knowing in us is born, it is by faith that we are just absolutely certain of its existence. There is no room for doubt.

We can never underestimate the power of our faith. No, we can't!

It is by faith that we understand in our own limited way the Holy Trinity of God.

Now, our souls rejoice within us when faith in Jesus Christ is born. We have heart-singing joy inside because our souls know the Truth (Jesus) already. We came from God. Our souls know God, and Jesus is God in the flesh! And it is the Truth (Jesus) who sets us free from that big, old, gaping, empty hole inside of us that constantly keeps us searching for something to fill it. We find out that it is not something that can fill it, but it is someone! Jesus sets us free from the search because He is the one who can fill that hole in us. Yes, He can. Why is that? It is because the hole, that special place inside of us, belongs strictly to Him. It is a holy hole! There is absolutely nothing else in this whole wide world and nobody else in this world that can fill this particular hole, because it is His home. When God made us, He made room for Himself inside of us! He then gave us free will to decide if we want Him in our lives. He wants our love. Our love for Him is that important to Him. He wants genuine love, a wonderful, abundant relationship and fellowship with us. He wants to walk and talk with us on a daily basis. He doesn't want to control us. That's why He gave us free will. He wants us to decide for ourselves if this is what we want. There is eternal beauty in loving someone because we want to ... not because we feel we have to because they are demanding it. That doesn't work. It doesn't work in our earthly relationships with each other, and it doesn't work with God because He made us in His own image. We are like Him. It is our own choice if we want that hole filled with what it was made for. He wants and hopes to be chosen out of love.

I made that choice when I was ten years old. At church one day, I felt Him knocking on the door to His room in me, and I could hardly wait to walk down that aisle and give Him His room. I opened that door and said, "Yes, Jesus, please, please come in and live with me; I want you." As I walked down that aisle, I remember feeling as if I were floating, not walking. I didn't even think my feet were touching the floor. That was because after I took that first step toward Him, He came running with joy to meet me, and He walked with me as I professed my faith in Him and to Him in front of all those present. I felt tears of joy and completeness. He moved in with me at that very moment. (He didn't waste any time!) He will move in with you too right now, if you haven't asked Him to as of yet. All you have to do is ask Him to come into your heart because you want Him. He has just been waiting for the invitation. That place inside of us was made there by God for Jesus to live in, for God to live in, for the Holy Spirit to live in. To think they want to live in me. I just want to jump up and down, stomp my feet with joy, dance, sing, and clap my hands! I brought my mind, heart, and soul together in total unity that day when I took that first step of faith. I didn't have to do anything but believe and say, "Yes, I believe that Jesus is the Christ, the Son of the living God, and I invite Him to come live with me." I said it with all of my mind, all my heart, and all my soul ("Yes, yes, yes!"). That was three yeses (mind, heart, and soul).

God did the rest of it. He pulled it all together because of my surrendering to this great and wondrous faith. In fact, He even provided the faith. It was there all the time. All I had to do was claim it. He provided everything I needed and still does.

That was just the beginning. A few days later, our church met at the Chaplin River where I was led down into the water to be baptized as Jesus was baptized by His cousin, John the Baptist (Matthew 3:13–17). It was there that I received a gift. It was a gift sent directly from heaven. I received the gift of the Holy Spirit (Acts 2:38).

I became so rich because now all of heaven moved in with me. I was only ten years old, and I loved the Lord and His church with all my heart. I have never left my faith, but there have been many times that I have failed in my Christian walk. I know there have been many times that I have grieved the Holy Spirit who lives in me because I have not always obeyed, and I have reaped many consequences of my willful ways. The fact that my Father in heaven loves me enough to let me reap what I sow makes me want to weep with a thankful heart. This is called pruning and refining of my soul and brings me closer to Him and His ways. I am not there yet, by no means, and won't be until I have breathed my last breath and go to live with Him. I have much learning to do. Living the Christian life will always be a growing experience. I think the Christian life is so exciting! How could it not be? What could be better than walking and talking with God the Creator of the universe?! Praise His holy name!

It is wonderful, but that doesn't mean it is easy. Sometimes, it is far from easy. Let's get real. It hasn't been easy for anybody. This is powerful information for us to know and accept. Life isn't always easy and never will be on this earth. We have an enemy called Satan. He wants us to forget about God. He wants us to forget that Jesus lives inside of us, and he wants us to forget that the Holy Spirit is our gift. This means he goes to war with our souls. Christians are in big-time war with the devil, and he is ready to attack at any given moment. We must be alert to this. He can't stand us. He is our enemy. Well, what does he want? He wants to stop our testimony, our good Christian name, our witnesses as servants of Jesus. He wants to mar us in front of the world. And he wants us to suffer in our personal lives. He does this by luring us into getting our priorities out of order. He wants us to concentrate only on ourselves and our flesh desires. He wants us to disobey God so that we will not live the abundant life that God desires for us.

This puts us as big old number one and in front of God. This leads to disaster, and Satan loves disaster for us. This enemy of ours wants to lead us astray as much as possible; he is relentless. He always wants us to think that the grass is greener on the other side, and he will constantly pull us toward jumping the fence only to find out, as Eve did, that it is not greener at all; sometimes it is even brown, and sometimes there is no grass at all, and we end up sitting in the dirt of our own making. That is the sad part of reaping the consequences that come with jumping the fence. However, these consequences are a Godsend! They are a Godsend just as they were to the prodigal son (Luke 15:11–31). What a beautiful story!

He had to learn the difference of what it meant to live the worldly life and the true life of his soul. In living it up with his ego in charge (and egos want to live the worldly life) in the end, it only brought emptiness to his heart, and it all meant nothing. It was then that he surrendered and let that old ego go, and he returned to the one who truly loved him and knew what was best for him. In doing this, he became whole in loving himself. He learned it the hard way, but he was sincere in his return, and he knew in his mind, heart, and soul that he was truly loving himself when he came back home.

We are the prodigal sons and daughters of God when we are led astray by Satan (none of us are immune to this happening), but God, our Father, waits with open arms to welcome us back when we are ready to confess, repent, and return like the prodigal son returned to his father.

The consequences of our actions can help us get back on the right track again and get our priorities back in order. Jesus says this order is found in the greatest commandment. We are to love God first (not ourselves) and love Him with everything we've got, our minds, our hearts, and our souls, and then love our neighbors as we love ourselves (Matthew 22:36–39).

I have included this in my introduction to be honest with you in saying that I know I have been a prodigal daughter many times. Satan tricks me and lures me with his bait when I am blind and unaware, vulnerable or self-righteous, in the depths of pain and or in the heights of happiness. It doesn't matter to him because anywhere he can sense an opening, a crack, he uses it. He comes like a thief in the night. He came to Peter when Peter was in a lot of emotional pain. Peter was scared, vulnerable, and trapped. Jesus had told Peter that he would deny him. Peter declared that it wouldn't happen. He said he would die with Christ before he would ever disown him. The other disciples said the same thing (Matthew 26:35 NIV).

But it happened.

Oh no!

It happens. God knows it is going to happen. God always welcomes us back when we realize what we have done. He loves us so much; His compassion and mercy know no bounds. Nothing can separate us from this great love that He has for us.

In Romans 8:38–39 (NIV) Paul says, "For I am convinced that neither death nor life, neither angels nor demons, neither the present nor the future, nor any powers, neither height nor depth, nor anything else in all creation, will be able to separate us from the love of God that is in Christ Jesus our Lord."

Wow! There is not one thing that can separate me from the love of God that is in Christ Jesus our Lord. Nothing! God has always welcomed me back after reaping the consequences of my actions, or my conscience has burned with guilt until I have opened my eyes to the truth (or the cock crows) and been honest with Him about my shortcomings, weaknesses, and sins. And like Peter, I go out and weep bitterly for my sins. God has compassion and mercy for us, His children. He uses all of this and helps me grow stronger from all my experiences and start all over. As Christians, we are saints of God who are in constant spiritual battle. He knows the spiritual war we are in and that we cannot win it without His help. He knows we fail to be on guard, and we get attacked and wounded when we least expect it. But it is all for a reason. God knows what we need to become strong Christians in His army. He knew what was ahead of Peter and how Peter had to be sifted, molded, and refined to do the job that was planned for him to do. Things haven't changed. We come back stronger soldiers than ever when we learn our lessons from the battlefield of life. The answer lies in never giving up the faith through our struggles. We earn many purple hearts during our battles. We just don't know it because we can't physically see them, but one day we will receive the crown of life. Our crowns at this point are invisible, but they are there all the same. I picture the crown on my head, the purple hearts on my chest as I get up time and time again. We will be victorious for eternity when we continually submit to the Savior because Jesus has already won the war.

In 2 Timothy 4:7–8 (NIV), Paul said:
"I have fought the good fight, (Oh, yes, it's a fight but a good one.)
I have finished the race, (Yay!)
I have kept the faith. (Yay!)
Now there is in store for me the crown of righteousness, (How wonderful!)
which the Lord, the righteous Judge, will award to me on that day—
and not only to me,
but also to all who have longed for his appearing." (Oh, thank you, Lord!)

The Christian life is a fight in this world, but it is a good fight. We fight the evil one with God as our commander in chief. Jesus has already won the war, so we fight with confidence. We keep the faith, and we long for His appearing.

The Holy Trinity is invisible, yet the Great Three in One is in us and all around us and always at work. We just can't see Him with physical eyes. Not yet. The fact is, however, that we can see, feel, and know with our spiritual eyes and ears, hearts, and souls because He speaks to our spirits, and that is who we really are.

God came to me, allowing me to commune with the invisible, revealing to me that heaven and earth are one. I did not see any of this with my physical eyes but with the eyes of my spirit, who is the real me, who dwells in this house, which is my body.

'We are part of the whole eternal spiritual picture. We are one with it. I am not talking about the city of heaven, our future eternal home. I am talking about the heavenly realm that is all around us and in us.

Jesus said for us to love God first and with everything we've got. Then we are to love our neighbors as we love ourselves (Matthew 22:37 NIV).

How do we possibly achieve all this loving? He makes it possible for us to achieve all this loving through faith in Him. When we have faith in Him, He can work through us, which makes Him our leader and guide, and He can *lead* us to the loving.

Hebrews 11:6 (NIV):
"And without faith it is impossible to please God, (Impossible.)
because anyone who comes to him
must believe that He exists (We have to have faith in Him.)

and that He rewards those who earnestly seek him." (Oh, thank you, our Lord God!)

This faith is called sweet surrender to the one who created us and knows us in every way possible. We are to love ourselves, and this surrender is the most powerful way that we show love to our own selves! Oh, how sweet! Oh, how sweet! Oh, how sweet! I just can't say it enough. This sweet surrender enhances every detail of our lives, and we are enriched. We have found the pot at the end of the rainbow.

This book is about pain and sorrow. You may shed some tears. Oh, yes, there's lots of pain. But that's not all. This book is about faith, hope, and love. Your soul may sing, rejoice, and feel like dancing! This book is about all these things, but the greatest thing this book is about is love. God loves the world. Love starts with God. He is Love. He loves us. You are my neighbor. I love God, and I love you as I love myself, and I am here to share with you.

> And now these three remain:
> faith, hope and love.
> But the greatest of these is love.
> —1 Corinthians 13:13

Part II

LIFE CHANGED

JEREMY AND DUSTIN

It was beautiful springtime in May 1996 when it happened. It was the time of breathtaking paradise with gorgeous, warm days and lovely blue skies in the bluegrass state of Kentucky. Green grass was growing like crazy, which meant mowing it a lot, sometimes twice a week to keep it looking wonderful. And, oh, the flowers—they were blooming everywhere with their blossoms adding color and fragrance to the sweet, clean air. People were buying and planting flowers, hanging flower baskets and ferns on front porches and back decks, and filling flowerpots. The birds were singing and rejoicing as they went about their business of building nests, getting ready for their families. Farmers on their tractors were pulling plows that were breaking ground, opening up the fresh, earthy scent of dirt and getting it ready for all the gardens and tobacco patches. School would soon be out, and summer was on its way. I just love my home state of Kentucky. It is absolutely wonderful to me to be able to experience its beauty and uniqueness. It is all so *splendid*!

Dustin was our new grandbaby at the time, almost six months old. Our daughter, Julie, and our son-in-law, Brian, were brand-new parents. Dustin was our first grandchild, and he was absolutely delightful, and wonderful, and squeezable, and lovable; well, all of you grandparents know how it is! Someone had told me one time, "There are no words to describe the feelings you have when a grandchild is born." I found out what a true statement that is. I was astonished at these newly acquired feelings that came with the new grandbaby. They seemed to be a package deal delivered at the very same time. I praised God for the wonderful and holy God that He is to give us such gifts as grandchildren. Dustin was a marvel to behold and brought incredible joy to us because he was an extension of ourselves. We belonged together in the blessed, God-given bond between grandchild and grandparents.

Our teenage son, Jeremy, had gone to "Thunder over Louisville" for the first time in his life and had been so excited and thrilled over it that he couldn't quit talking about it. He had stood on one of the bridges that connect Kentucky and Indiana as boom after boom of fireworks lit up the Louisville sky and shook the bridge beneath his feet. That was the most excited I had ever seen him, and it was wonderful seeing him so happy.

Jeremy really enjoyed Dustin's company too. Jeremy was seventeen years old. He was big, strong, masculine, and of course, in my opinion, very handsome. When Dustin was at our house, Jeremy would sometimes take him into his room for some one-on-one time. Jeremy had a couch in his bedroom, and they sat on the couch together, with Jeremy holding him in his arms and telling him all kinds of stuff boys ought to know. I know this because the door was wide open, and it was a pleasure to see them sitting there. Now, they did not talk out loud. It was not measured by Dustin's age or what was actually being said. Most of the time, there was nothing being said. Dustin just sat in Jeremy's lap looking around, and both of them were silently thinking together and of course listening to music. Music was one of Jeremy's passions. He loved music. He loved speakers, sound systems, and experimenting with any kind of musical equipment. One time he even took the radio out of my car! Oh, yes, it's true. He thought I needed a better one. I agreed to let him do this, and I went without a radio for a brief time while he worked on it. Speakers were very important to Jeremy. He had an ear for music. Troy, one of his cousins, has this same love. They got it from my daddy, who has loved music for as long as I can remember and even way before I was born. When I was growing up, Momma would read the Bible to us (my brother, Ricky, my sister, Karen, and me) before bedtime, and then Daddy would put a record on the record player, and we went to bed with music playing on the stereo. By the time the record was finished, we were sound asleep.

Okay, back to Jeremy and Dustin. I knew Jeremy was a good uncle. I knew He and Dustin were going to have so much fun together as Dustin grew up. I felt happy about this. Happy tears would well up in my eyes just thinking about their present and future relationship together.

As always, there was so much involved in just keeping things going in the day-to-day living. You know how it is. Where does the time go? Life was moving fast. Added to that, we were preparing for Jeremy's high school graduation. The invitations were right there on the kitchen counter by the back door, stamped and ready to be put in the mail. The graduation gown was hanging proudly in the doorway for all to see, waiting to be pressed, and the cap was displayed right over by the invitations. We started planning a graduation party with Jeremy's cousin, Lisa. She was his cousin on his father's side of the family. Lisa's mom, Alice, is Billy's sister. Lisa was in the same graduation class as Jeremy, and so was his cousin Davy from my side of the family. Davy's dad, Ricky, is my brother. We were planning on going to Davy's graduation party too. There was so much to celebrate! It was such an exciting event coming up for us and for both sides of our families at the very same time. Jeremy had always been close cousins with Davy and Lisa. Actually, Julie and Jeremy were close to all of their cousins on both sides of our family, especially those close to their own ages.

Before I go any further, I have something to confess. In all this whirlwind of everyday activity, I had a problem staying in the present moment. Being a working mom and keeping the home fires burning took a lot of energy. I would be doing one thing, but my mind would be on many other things. It took a lot of juggling and multitasking with several things that I needed to do, so there was always a lot on my mind, or so it seemed. It also seemed like even more things came pushing in on me, like things that happened in the past, or things that might happen in the future, or something I was worried about in the present. The villain of all this brain activity is Satan. He torments us about all of it ... past, present, and future. He doesn't really care which one he can use, just so he can torment us about something ... everything ... and anything except enjoying and doing our best in the present moment. I was pretty naïve about his ways. There were lots of things I didn't know, and this included how the brain works. There were always thoughts that would crowd in on me that were not mine. They would drive me absolutely crazy, but at the time, I didn't know they weren't mine. These thoughts were thieves robbing me of peace of mind.

They were robbing me of my present moments. The problem was that I was actually *mindless* of what was going on in my very own mind. Since I didn't even know they were robbing me, I didn't do anything to try to stop them. It was like sitting and watching TV while people carry everything you own out the door, and you just sit there oblivious to it. And that was happening every day. Satan was carrying my present moments out the backdoor and replacing them with all kinds of other things without any resistance from me. This included worrying, stewing, and wondering. My mind was controlling me when I should have been controlling my mind! This was not a good thing. How could it be?

Jesus says to "love God with all your mind." Isn't that right? Well, I had not studied that enough, had not pondered it enough, and had not learned how to do that. Also, I have learned that lack of certain vitamins or other physical problems in the body can cause the brain to not want to shut down, which makes it harder to control. Sometimes, I have been powerless with my own mind because it did not have the nourishment it needed to work successfully. I know this is true because I have experienced it. Our bodies are so uniquely wired that any problem in the body can affect other parts. Our physical health is very important for living a Christian life. Satan can use our physical weaknesses against us, so we have to work hard at keeping all our parts healthy, including our brain.

Even with a healthy brain, what we *think* has a super impact on how we feel, what actions we take, how we sleep, how happy or unhappy we are, and so on. That is why the Bible tells us what we have to do to help control our thoughts.

In 2 Corinthians 10:5 (NIV), it says, "We demolish arguments and every pretension that sets itself up against the knowledge of God, and we take captive every thought to make it obedient to Christ."

Whew! Now that's a big job to do. These arguments and pretensions are started in our minds by our enemy, but we are supposed to be soldiers who recognize them and take them captive by taking them to Jesus Christ and letting Him lead us by doing what He says about each and every thought. We can talk it over with our Lord. Jesus will help us chase the negative thoughts away. Faith and hope are our helpers. We believe and know He will help us. Positive attitude and positive thinking are powerful tools. We don't have to let Satan get by with manipulating our brains. They're our brains—not his! The Bible is our sword in this spiritual warfare. We are soldiers with a sword. This is another example of how I can use my faith keys to unlock the treasures that will assist me in this battle. Satan will lie to me and steal from me, and I have to know when he is lying and stealing. Of course, we know it's an ongoing battle.

I hadn't studied how to be the soldier in my own mind, and I hadn't taken very good care of my health, so my mind was very good at this trickery. However, here we were in May 1996 when things changed. Everything—and I mean everything—every ... little ... thing ... came to a mind-stopping, brake-slamming, screeching, screaming halt. My unbridled mind was thrown into shock. I was jerked to the present moment, and I stayed right there. Nothing else mattered.

I was screaming in my mind to God to help me.

"Oh, my dear, dear, dear, God in heaven ... oh, my Father in heaven, help me, please, please help me ... they tell me Jeremy is dead. My Savior and my God, I can't stand it. Oh ... Father God, help me, help me, I pray. Help me, help me, help me, please, please, please help me."

Our son was gone.

Julie's brother was gone.

Brian's brother-in-law was gone.

Dustin's uncle was gone.

Grandparents lost their grandchild. He was gone.

Aunts and uncles lost their nephew.

Cousins lost their cousin.

Friends lost their friend.

I felt lost, disconnected, flung out, and splintered. I was about to start on a journey that I didn't want to be on, but God rescued me from the pit of agony and despair. Rescuing me did not mean that He took away my pain. Oh no, He did not. He brought me *through* the pain. He carried me. He led me. He pulled me. He pushed me. He held me. He rocked me. He spoke to me through His Word. He spoke to me through people in the Bible. He spoke to me through my friends and family. He spoke to me through my loved ones who had already passed on to glory. He spoke to me through books. He spoke to me through nature. He spoke to me through daily living.

The only way I was going to get over the pain was to plow through it to get to the other side of it. He knew it had to be done. He didn't spare me from it, but He got me through it. When I was ten, He had given me the gift of the Holy Spirit, who is also called the Comforter. He never left me. The Holy Trinity, the Father, Son, and Holy Spirit, all worked to get me through the pain.

2 Corinthians 1:3 (NIV):
"Praise be to the God and Father of our Lord Jesus Christ,
the Father of compassion
and the God of all comfort, (the God of what? He is the God of *all* comfort!)
who comforts us in all our troubles, (Comforts us in what? He comforts us in *all* our troubles, not just some of them but *all* of them!)
(Why?)
so that we can comfort those in any trouble (So we can do what? Comfort those in *any* kind of trouble! What do we comfort them with?)
with the comfort we ourselves have received from God."

It is my hope and prayer that my testimony of surviving the most horrible devastation I have experienced on earth, which is having my child die before me, can comfort you somehow, no matter what you are going through. I hope that my experiences of how God comforted me will comfort you in your trouble no matter what your trouble might be.

Jesus said, "Blessed are those who mourn, for they will be comforted" (Matthew 5:4 NIV).

We don't know what true comfort means until we agonizingly need it. When it does come, we know we are truly being blessed by Almighty God the Father, whether it comes from God or from others who have been comforted by God, and they know how to comfort us. It is a gift from God either way.

I started this chapter out with Jeremy and Dustin. I have to say that one of my most blessed memories is seeing Jeremy sitting in his room on his couch holding Dustin in his lap. I can bring that picture of them to the forefront of my mind, and I can hold it there for as long as I like. Nothing can ever take that away from me. It is a moment caught in time that will live in my heart forever and ever. I know that Jeremy was starting out being a good uncle and knew what it took to have a relationship with his nephew. It took taking time to be with him. I know that Jeremy would have been a wonderful father if his life had not been cut short. Even though he didn't get the chance to experience his own children, I will always remember him holding Dustin close and being comfortable with it. This picture in my mind gives me much pleasure, and I smile through the tears.

Jeremy lives on through his nephew through the bloodline of heredity. There are many times that Dustin reminds me of Jeremy in so many different ways. Many people think that Dustin even looks like him. He lives on through Dustin in a physical sense that is so comforting, and I can only say, "God is so good."

I remember shortly after Jeremy's death that Julie and Dustin were at our house, and Julie found me in the bathroom crying very hard. It had swept over me again that Dustin would never know Jeremy.

I remember her telling me that this was not true. She said that even though Jeremy was gone physically, she would make sure that her children knew all about him, and he would always be a part of their lives in growing up. Julie and Brian have done a fine job of doing this for their children, and it feels good and as complete as it can be under the circumstances.

I am blessed to have a grandson like Dustin. He is an absolute gift to me, and I thank God for him being in my life. It is hard to believe that Dustin is all grown up now. He has flown to Poland for several years in a row with his church group to do mission work there. He has also gone on other mission trips to help people in need. He loves the Lord and His church, His missions, and His work. He has a red Silverado truck that I absolutely love. It has big red lights on the top of it because he is a volunteer fireman. He is going to school to be a professional firefighter. He is a night supervisor at a factory in a town about thirty minutes from his home. The biggest thrill of all is that Dustin is the father of Jase, a beautiful baby boy. Jeremy is now a great-uncle!

I know that Jeremy stays close to Dustin and watches him from our heavenly home. I know that Jeremy is in that cloud of witnesses who watch from above and cheer us on as we continue in this earthly life. I know that he is still very much a part of our lives and always and forever will be. I know that Jeremy will always be Dustin's uncle and close to him. I know he is helping cheer Dustin on in this race of life that is marked out for him.

We are told about this great cloud of witnesses. The twelfth chapter of Hebrews talks about the saints of old from our rich history who are still with us, watching us and witnessing out Christian journey.

Hebrews 12:1 (NIV):
"Therefore, since we are surrounded (Surrounded? Surrounded by what?) by such a great cloud of witnesses, (Oh, that's wonderful!)
let us throw off everything that hinders (Lord, please show me what hinders me.)
and the sin that so easily entangles, (Please help me let go of sin in me.)
and let us run with perseverance (Oh, Lord, help me hang in there.)
the race marked out for us." (Yes, Lord, I want to run the race you have marked for me.)

I look up into the sky. I visualize all these witnesses, and I know beyond a shadow of a doubt that I am surrounded with love and encouragement. I can see with spiritual eyes and feel them smiling really big because I am acknowledging their presence with me. I see Dustin putting on his running suit and running with perseverance the race that God has marked out for him, and I see Jeremy running right alongside Dustin.

> There is a time for everything,
> and a season for every activity under Heaven:
> a time to be born
> and a time to die.
> —Ecclesiastes 3:1–2 (NIV)

ETERNITY

At the time, it actually seemed as if the whole world had just put on its brakes and stopped. It just wasn't twirling anymore. No, it wasn't. It was standing absolutely still. Everything was at a standstill, and along with it, my life seemed to stop too. I had come to the end. It was the end of my life as I knew it. I was thrown, pitched, hurled into a different world. It was a world that I was not prepared for and, in all reality, could *never* be prepared for. It felt like a horrible, devastating nightmare that I was experiencing, but unfortunately I was awake. There was no escape from it. I could not wake up from it as if it was a nightmare because it was truth. It was then that I was forced to live in the present moment, due to the excruciating pain. *Nothing else mattered.* It was a matter of surviving from one day to the next, and many times, from one minute to the next.

Right smack dab in the middle of starting this new relationship and exciting walk with Dustin, a baby who still had the sweet, sweet smell of heaven all over him, we were handed a bomb that exploded in our hearts, giving us no choice but to stare death right in the face.

There it was: Dustin, a relatively new life, and Jeremy, a new death. One came down from heaven, and one went back up to heaven.

My bleeding heart was ripped wide open, exposed to the truth that this is the way our earthly life works. We are born, we live, and we die. I knew all this in my mind of course, but never had that truth been so stark, so real, so revealing.

My ever-wondering mind started to imagine that if I got up, went and got a bucket, put one drop of water in that bucket, and then looked down at that drop of water, I would be able to barely see it. Even as I imagine this in my mind, I also know it is truth. I have seen a drop of water fall into an empty bucket before. I have looked down at it, asking myself, "Where did it go?"

I felt like that was what I was doing. I was looking down (actually staring down) into that bucket to find that tiny drop of water. Jeremy's short life seemed like that tiny drop of water.

Jeremy was gone. Seventeen years of living was such a short life.

"Where did the years go?" I asked myself.

I even answered myself, "I don't know. I simply don't know."

We were not finished being with him. He did not get to graduate. Graduation was only in two weeks, and then he had the rest of his life before him. Except now, seventeen years was all he had.

There would be no more.

It was over.

I did know, though, that he was now starting his life in eternity. This part of his life would *never* have an end.

I went back to thinking about that tiny drop of water. I thought about comparing this earthly journey to that one drop of water. Is our earthly journey even as big as a drop of water compared to eternity?

Should I use something smaller than a drop of water? Should I imagine throwing that tiny drop of water out into the universe instead of in a bucket? Would that give me a better idea of life's timeline compared to eternity?

Thinking it through, I know that none of it would work. I will never find anything, nor will anybody else, to measure with or against eternity. It is an impossible feat because there is no measurement to eternity. I can't measure something that has no end.

However, this tiny drop of time spent on this earth is of paramount importance! Even though the timeline of it is microscopic compared to eternity, it is wonderful, powerful, meaningful, and monumental.

We live!

How do I keep something as fragile as this short, temporary earthly-life in perspective compared to the endless time of eternal life and still know that this tiny, minute amount of time is crucial to my spiritual development and precious in God's sight?

The writer Paul states that we can only see a part of the whole picture while we are here on this earth. We cannot see who we really are and what our being is all about, and we only understand a little bit about God and His ways. He compares it to looking into a mirror that is hazy and blurred. We can't see everything clearly and as it is, but someday we will. He says that now we only know part of it, but then we will know all of it (1 Corinthians 13:12).

My mind took off again thinking that as far as our earthly life is concerned, birth brings joy, and death brings pain. I felt the unspeakable joy when Dustin was born, and I felt the agonizing, gut-wrenching, unspeakable pain when Jeremy died.

I was reminded about Jeremy's high school English journal that his teacher gave to us. In his last year of high school, Jeremy wrote about emotions. He said we would be mere robots if we did not have emotions. He was so right! Robots are fine, but I don't want to be one. We would not even know love if we did not have emotions. Emotions are super important. God thinks so. He gave them to us.

God made us with emotions and feelings. He made us like Him! He has emotions and feelings too. When I read the Bible, I find out that there are times when God is pleased, times He is angry, times He is sad, times He delights in me, and times He wants to discipline me for my own good. Emotions are a part of who we are because we are like our Father. Yes, we are! There is no use in denying, shoving, stuffing, or ignoring them. They are as important as the rest of our being and should be honored and dealt with in a healthy way. Emotions should work for us. We should not work for them! We are the employer, and emotions are our employees. I learned pretty quickly that I was going to have to become friends with my emotions to survive. This was super important.

We experience the whole realm of living here, and while we learn from the physical aspect of this world, at the same time we are learning and growing in our spirits. It all works together. It is the most splendid and magnificent marvel to study how we are made and how we work. It is a never-ending study. Something new is always popping up. We grow physically, mentally, emotionally, and spiritually, and it will all go to heaven with us except the physical, which we don't need.

I knew all this in my mind. I knew what I believed. I knew Jeremy would get a brand-new wonderful body some sweet day, but oh, what a mess I was in. My emotions were splintered with the pain of losing him on this earth. I had to put all those emotions to good use so I could heal. I knew there was only one way for me to do that, and that way was to put God first and let Him lead me through the turbulent waters of my shattered emotions.

Therefore, it was in the midst of the agonizing pain of losing Jeremy that God met me. He came to me. His amazing love, mercy, and compassion went way beyond my understanding.

God knew my pain. Of course, He knows everything about everything. That's no big secret. But that is not all. He experienced earthly pain Himself as a Father when He sent His only begotten Son to live on earth for a short while.

His child had died too.

DEATH IS THE BRIDGE

I thought I knew the love I had for my children. Oh, yes, I did. I loved them so much I could squeeze them to pieces. I was a real worrywart over them, hovering just like a little ole mother hen. I was ridiculous about it sometimes. However, as loving as I thought I was, I didn't have a clue, was not aware of how deep that love resided in my soul until Jeremy was physically gone. No, I didn't. It was then that I realized with intense, gut-wracking pain that the parent-love is very deep. In fact, it is so deep … the end of it is unreachable. I can't reach the end of it, because there is no end to it! There is no end to love.

That's not all that happened. It reached so far within me that it went to a place I didn't even know existed. I am still in awe over this place that is inside of me that I didn't know about. It reached my very core. It went to that part of me that belongs to God, that place where I am one with God. It went beyond my mind, beyond my heart, all the way down into the depths of my soul, and there I found that word "unending" again. I learned something else. There is no end to my soul either! Therefore, there is no end to the love that is there. My soul will never die, so there is no end to me, and there is no end to my love! Unending was beyond my knowing! How could I have ever known of this place without experiencing it? I was anguished that I was experiencing it and shocked at its existence!

There was purity in that love that I was feeling. It is where God's love lives in me, and it is a wellspring of everlasting love that has no end! It is the well within just like Jesus explained to the woman at the well! This was astonishing to actually find this within myself! When Jesus moved in, He dug this well in me that never runs dry and has no end! He filled it completely to overflowing. Understanding flooded my soul! This was the spiritual joy I found; however, this did not take away the physical pain of separation. No, that didn't happen at all. The physical pain of separating Jeremy's spirit and my spirit from this place inside of me was unthinkable. The excruciating pain was mixed in with the unending love I have for my son. I learned something else about this newfound wellspring of love. Back during those occasions when my mind would take to stewing, worrying, binging, fretting, whatever you want to call it, I would start wondering if I loved God enough; if I did enough, was I good enough? I got my answer to that when I learned the depth of love I have for my children. I learned the depth of love I have for my God. Oh my, I was speechless. My love for God has no end. His love for me has no end. I knew in my heart that only death could teach me such depth. Only death could reach into the unending realm of love because death is the bridge from this world to the next. Death opens up new territory. I had my hand on this bridge, because part of me had died when my son died. Heaven became sweeter to me than ever before—so sweet I could almost taste it. Heaven and earth became united in a way I had never known before. Everything changed in the blink of an eye, and it was then that part of me went to heaven too.

How do I know this? I know this because part of me was gone, and that part went with Jeremy. It was then that I understood how much I was physically united with the heavenly kingdom because I have a son residing there. He came from my body. Even though our physical bodies do not go to heaven, our physical bodies are united with our spirits in an intricate way, making us who we are and who we always will be. This is beyond mortal understanding. He was knit together in me, part of me and part of his father. He is part of my everlasting soul. His sister, Julie, is part of him, and he is a part of her. Not only that, he is a part of all his earthly kinship and community friends. He joined some of them in heaven, and he left some of them on earth.

Even though I can't see it, I know there is a great link between those who have passed on and those of us who are still here on earth. This chain is broken physically because we can't see it but never spiritually. It's just invisible. My faith allows me to believe in the invisible with all my heart. Thank you, God!

Love continues on in a totally different way. We have a new kind of connection that is real and abiding. I rejoice that all my loved ones, family, and friends who have gone from this life are still alive. In fact, they are more alive than ever! They are sparkling in God's presence!

I look at death differently now than I did before. Wait. Let me think. What I mean to say is that I *feel* different about it now. I have always believed in heaven, but I didn't know what it would *feel* like to have a child there. Feeling and believing are two very different things. One comes from my mind, and the other comes from my heart. Both are important. Jeremy went home. I knew that in my mind, but feeling the power of this new connection added to my longing to go home. I am just a visitor here; this place is temporary. Feeling added to the dimension of knowing. Knowing is good. Feeling is good.

Jeremy had crossed the bridge of death that leads home. He got there before I did, but I had my hand on this bridge, and he held out his hand from this bridge. We clasped hands. We are linked together forever even though we are physically apart for now. We are in the land of the invisible. His hand is reaching down, and my hand is reaching up. Our spiritual hands are clasped, and one day ... oh, one sweet day ... when that bridge opens up to me, the rest of me will join him, never to be apart again.

MY GRIEF

Grief was nothing new to me. I had felt it before when other loved ones had died, but it became brand-new to me when Jeremy died. It hit me personally where it hurt the most, and it took years for me to get through it. It was heavy, oh, so very heavy. My grief could not be lifted all at once. No, it couldn't. It was way too overwhelming. I had to honor it and treat it ever so gently and patiently. Grief takes as much time as it needs. It does not just go away. It demands attention. It cannot be rushed. It cannot be swept away as if nothing is wrong unless, of course, if God chooses to make it that way. This was my time to grieve, and there was nothing that could make it any better. Once it had attacked that place that runs so deep within me, you know that place I am talking about, that place that was secretly made inside of me, it had to run its own course. Jeremy was not here anymore. That cold, hard fact was hard to accept. It was hard to endure. Nothing could bring him back. Nothing, not one absolute thing, was going to bring him back.

There were no quotes in the Bible that anyone could say to me that helped my *physical* pain. There were times I didn't want to hear them. Let me tell you why. I knew what was in the Bible, and I believed it. This helped my *spiritual* pain, but it did not help my *physical* pain of separation. That pain was still there. If I did not have this hope of the Bible, then that would have been a different story. I would have thirsted for those words. I would have needed them for my spiritual sanity. I cannot comprehend or fathom what it would have been like if I had not had this security and this hope that held me together. I knew Jeremy was okay, and because of my belief in the Bible, I had hope and faith that I would see him again. I *knew* I would see him again. This was healing balm for my tortured soul. Words from the Bible strengthened my spirit, yet for my physical suffering, words had no meaning. This pain was too deep for words. There were no words in this whole wide world that could make me feel better physically.

There was only one thing that I needed for my physical pain and torture, and that one thing was love. I needed the verb love that showed action. I am talking about the love that is described in 1 Corinthians, chapter 13. I needed the real love that consists of lots of patience that allowed me to grieve in any way I needed to. I needed the real love that is full of kindness that helped to take care of my physical needs when I couldn't take care of myself. I needed the real love that would cry with me, laugh with me, sit with me, and listen to me. I needed the real kind of love that shows itself through giving, caring, and sharing. This is the real love derived from the Holy Spirit, showing its fruit, called patience, goodness, gentleness, kindness, and faithfulness (Galatians 5:22).

It was what I needed, and it was what I got. We had all the labor of the Holy Spirit's fruit of love. In fact, we were surrounded by it, enclosed by it, and protected by it. We had two wonderful families who loved us very much. Even though they were completely devastated themselves in their grief, they tenderly cared for us. Each one in his and her way poured out compassion beyond the call of duty. They walked the extra mile. There are no words to express the beauty of love exhibited by and from these two families. They treated us with great love, honor, and respect while we grieved and while they grieved too. We grieved together. The caring love that we received was widespread, including people from our communities throughout the county. Friends are essential, and we had and still have the best kind. Our friends walked the extra mile too.

We are supposed to grieve. God made us this way, and as we grieve, we have hope and not despair. We all knew we would see Jeremy again. We were united in love as we grieved together, and that love factor made us to be sweet perfume to God above.

Part III

BETWEEN HEAVEN AND EARTH

THE SWORD OF DEATH

The sword of death struck my heart on May 19, 1996.

I will start with the beginning of the day before the nineteenth, which was a Saturday. We had a day trip planned for that day. My parents, Julie, and Dustin were going with us on a road trip to the eastern part of Kentucky. We were going to take in the beauty of the mountains and drink in some of that wonderful, fresh mountain spring air. I was excited about this trip because I love the mountains. I just stare at them in wonder and amazement at their beauty. Our son-in-law Brian couldn't go; he had to work. Jeremy didn't want to go. We weren't surprised that Jeremy didn't want to go because at his age, we knew he would rather be with his friends on a Saturday night. He had a fully scheduled day ahead. He had signed up for Saturday school until noon. This was because he had missed school several days due to having had strep throat twice before getting well. In the afternoon, he was going to work with his cousin Chad in their grandmother Connie's yard.

Jeremy was the first one to leave that Saturday morning. As he was going out the door, he looked back at us and at the last minute asked if he could spend the night with a friend.

I said, "No, not tonight."

He asked us what time we would be back from our trip to the mountains, and I said it would probably be around 1:00 a.m. That's what he had figured it would be. Jeremy's curfew was twelve, so he thought about that. His response seemed realistic.

He said, "Since you don't expect to be back earlier than that, why can't I just go on home with Joe?"

It was logical enough, so Billy and I both thought it would be okay for him to do that.

As he turned to leave, he looked back one more time and said, "I'll see you at church in the morning."

Well, we had a wonderful time that day on our trip to the mountains. Dustin was just six months old, but he did great and enjoyed himself. That was part of our joy that day. We found out later that Jeremy had a good day too. Days later, his cousin Chad came and told us all about their day together.

We got home around 1:00 a.m. just as we thought we would. I was so tired; I had no trouble falling asleep at all. Later, I'm not sure what time it was (I didn't look at the clock), I was suddenly wide awake. I didn't feel right at all. I sat up in the bed. Something was happening to me. I didn't know what it was. It felt like there was something inside me, besides me. I just knew there was something in me! I was bewildered to say the least. There was no pain, and I wasn't scared. I just didn't understand what was going on. I thought maybe I should wake Billy to tell him about this. I sat there in bed and wondered what to do. I just remember thinking, *What is in me?*

Then I thought differently about it. Why wake Billy when nothing was wrong? How was I going to explain it? What could I say that would make any sense to him? It sure didn't make any sense to me.

What is in me? I wondered over and over. As I was pondering what to do, the sensation left. It left quickly and lightly. Whatever it was, it seemed to be over. I was okay, so I lay back down and went right back to sleep.

The phone rang at 5:00 a.m. Scott, our minister, was calling. He said he must come to see us. Billy knew that something was terribly wrong, and he kept insisting that Scott tell him. Finally, Scott said that Jeremy had been killed in a car accident. Billy threw down the phone and started screaming. I immediately went into shock. I reminded Billy that Jeremy was spending the night with a friend. I comforted him by saying, "It can't be true."

Since my mind could not absorb this, I remained calm and reassuring. That is exactly how I felt. I said very calmly, "You'll see. When they get here, they'll tell us it isn't true."

We went in the living room to wait. I sat in a chair. Billy was on his knees by the chair and had put his head in my lap, and I was comforting him. I had no idea I was in shock. Scott, Leland, and Ken were at our door in minutes, but it didn't seem like even that long. It seemed like seconds to me. We were close friends with all three of these men, and they had to bear this horrible, devastating news to us. I couldn't accept it. No, I couldn't. The shock of it all was keeping me from absorbing the truth. I had completely shut down inside. It was as though someone had just taken a key and turned me off.

Ken, a friend from church, got on his knees, took my hand into his, looked me in the eyes, and kept repeating over and over that it was true. After some time, somehow he got through to me. When reality finally seeped in my brain, my first response was to beg them to pray. That's all I could think of. I knew we could not survive this on our own. I knew I needed God more than ever before in my entire life. All three men prayed, and then I said I wanted to pray. I remember praying and thanking God for giving Jeremy to us for seventeen years. The prayers were finished. What stood out most of all to me at that time (and at this time also) was when Ken prayed, "Dear Lord, you know their pain, because your Son died too." This stuck in my mind and heart in a way that it never had. After all, I had never experienced this kind of pain before.

Even though reality had come to me, and I had accepted the truth of it in my mind, I was still in shock. I just sat there in the chair after that, not really aware of my surroundings and what was going on. I had no idea where Billy was or what he was doing, and it didn't even occur to me to wonder about it. I was just vaguely aware that Scott, Ken, and Leland were still there. Scott was our minister, Ken was one of the elders of our church, and Leland was the youth minister from the Baptist church. Leland started calling our families.

My parents were the first to arrive, and when I saw them, it jerked me out of shock for a few moments, and I remember releasing deep, anguished sobs that I didn't recognize. The noise didn't even sound like me. These sobs came from that place inside me that I didn't know about, the place I told you about. It was that place I hadn't even known existed until now.

I didn't know who I was. I had been swallowed up by tragedy. It had come in a cruel attack that swallowed me up in an instant and consumed me. I knew then that part of me would be gone for the rest of my lifetime on this earth. The sword of death had struck my inner being. The sword of death had come swiftly and was accurately piercing in the center of my heart. It plunged deep, and I felt semiconscious with a sort of awareness. Shock and grief sent me spiraling to another world, one that I was not familiar with.

I kept thinking, *Who died? Was it me or was it Jeremy?* Confusion reigned. I wasn't sure, but I did know that part of me was gone.

There was nothing anyone could do. The sword was all the way through me.

> Since no man knows the future,
> who can tell him what is to come?
> No man has power over the wind to contain it,
> so no one has power over the day of his death.
> —Ecclesiastes 8:7 (NIV)

THE GOODBYE HUG

When my *mind* finally accepted the truth that Jeremy was dead, I knew, I simply knew. I knew deep down in my soul what I had experienced earlier that morning when I was awakened from a deep sleep.

I had known at the time that something was inside me besides me, but I didn't understand the feeling. When my mind accepted the truth, God opened my eyes to the fact that it was *Jeremy*. Jeremy's soul/spirit had entered me once again!

When his physical body had been knitting together inside of me before he was born, his soul/spirit had entered his body. There is no doubt about this fact. Therefore his body and his soul/spirit had been inside of me at the time he was forming in my womb.

After his physical body had died on that morning of May 19, he came to me to say goodbye. His soul/spirit had entered my body to give me a hug. God had allowed him to hug his mother goodbye and at the same time allowed me to feel that something was inside of me. His spirit hugged my spirit! His soul hugged my soul. It touches me deep inside even now as I write this. I am filled with love for the compassion I received that morning. It brings sweet tears of remembrance running down my face at this moment. What a gift it was from the glorious God that I serve.

I knew at the time there was something inside me besides me. I felt it, but I didn't understand it. To describe it a little more, I would say again that there was no pain; I had no anxiety, no feeling that anything was wrong. It was not just a feeling of fullness. It was a feeling of something extra being inside of me. It was in my neck, my chest and in both arms. It was in everything we use when we give a hug!

The timing of it was between the actual accident and the phone call telling of his death. I had been given a spiritual gift at that time that I would later recognize as a sign of unconditional love. This could not have happened without the permission from the Father to Jeremy and to me. It was a heart-to-heart gift. It was a miracle! Jeremy wanted to hug me goodbye and had asked for permission to do so, and God had granted him his request. I was allowed to feel him inside of me, and then God gave me the recognition of it later when I needed it. It would not have done any good if my spiritual eyes had not been opened. It would not have done any good if I had refused to accept the gift, but I grasped that gift with everything I had. I *knew* it was true. Jeremy didn't want to leave me, and he knew I could not go with him at this time, so he hugged me goodbye.

"Oh, God, I have no words! This is not something I can describe sufficiently! It is the most beautiful of all beautiful! All these years later, I still feel that hug, and I know, I know, I know that the angels *rejoiced* when I recognized that wonderful gift I had been given!"

Jeremy is not dead!

I just can't see him with my physical eyes.

He is invisible!

"Jesus, oh, Jesus, your miracles never end! You spoke of God's love while you were here on this earth. You performed miracles as the one and only Son of God. You taught us to pray, and you tell us in your Word how we are to love God. We are to love Him 100 percent with mind, heart, and soul. It means for me to love Him with everything that I am, my total being. Anything less is not enough. I understand more about this, because of what I have experienced! Oh, Jesus, I thank you with all of my mind, all my heart, and all my soul! Thank you for sending the Holy Spirit with Jeremy to give me such a heart-loving gift."

As I have already mentioned, death taught me the depth and the totality of the love I have for my children. As Jeremy's mom, that is how I had loved him, with all my mind, all my heart, and all of my soul, and as my son, that is how he had loved me, but we still didn't know how deep this love was. It is from a spiritual well of love that never runs dry. We didn't realize this depth during the time he was on this earth. We had never been to this sacred place. However, I knew it when our spirits united in a hug, and God opened my eyes about it later!

I know now that I have that same totality of love for my Lord too. This total love does not mean any of us are perfect. It does not mean that I am perfect and live a perfect life or that Jeremy was perfect and lived a perfect life because that is actually impossible. Only God is perfect. I have total love for my Lord, but it doesn't mean I have always put Him first. Challenges arise in my life and throw me off guard, as I have said before, and I mess up big time. He doesn't stop loving me though. He forgives me. This is the unconditional love He has for me … for all of us. He knows how hard it is. He knows my heart and knows I want to put Him first, but I fail many times. He still disciplines me, works with me, guides me, and teaches me so I can continually learn how to put Him first and mature in it. He pours mercy on me and loves me. That's why He died for me. That's why He died for you. I did not deserve it. I am a sinner saved by God's grace. I didn't deserve this spiritual goodbye hug either, but God granted Jeremy's request, and I received a precious, glorious gift from above.

When I found out about Jeremy's death, all of me, meaning my mind, my heart, and soul, was incorporated in the realization of what had happened to me early that morning. Why? So I could recognize the gift that I was being given when I woke up from a deep sleep the morning he died! My soul had the knowing of this truth, my mind accepted this knowing, my physical body had felt it when it happened, and my heart received it and said yes! There was no denying it. I was in complete agreement—mind, heart, and soul. My faith was unshakable on this.

God let me know that Jeremy would love me forever and would be waiting for me when my physical life here is over. The goodbye hug was a spiritual event that marked our physical separation. It was the very last hug that I received from Jeremy, and it is super special because it was his heavenly hug! I will hold the heavenly goodbye hug close to my heart always and forever.

God is mysterious. Praise His holy name!

"Thank you, God, my heavenly Father, for that priceless, heavenly gift you gave to me on that early, fateful morning of May 19, 1996 and thank you for your unconditional love."

Rhonda J. Goff

> As you do not know the path of the wind,
> Or how the body is formed in a mother's womb,
> so you cannot understand the work of God, the Maker of all things.
> —Ecclesiastes 11:5 (NIV)

THE GOLDEN RULE

Jesus covered so many topics in His teaching and preaching when He lived here. One of those rich verses from Him is very simple yet profound. He summed it up in what we call the golden rule. "So in everything, do to others what you would have them do to you, for this sums up the Law and the Prophets" (Matthew 7:12 NIV).

This statement is so powerful that He went on to say this very rule sums up the law. It sums up the prophets. Wow! We have one sentence to go by; we are good to go.

However, even though it sounds simple enough, sometimes, yes, many times, it can be so hard to do. Simple does not always mean easy.

My "self" has a way of getting in my own way because the golden rule goes beyond being nice when things are easy. Oh, yes, it does. There is no challenge when things are already going my way. I don't even have to get the golden rule out of the toolbox for that.

Using the golden rule is a skill, a practice, and a remembrance, and even with that being said, it usually does not come naturally, and quite frankly, I might as well admit it, I can't do it by myself. The Holy Spirit in me has to have control of me for it to work. He is my gift from God to help me do what I should do, but I have to willingly let Him work in me. If I let Him work through me, then I am in God's will. However, I will be the first to admit that my emotions can take control of me so easily that I forget that the golden rule should be in control. I realize that I am supposed to use the golden rule at all times, in bad as well as good. I am to stop and examine all experiences in a light pointed toward myself, asking myself this question:

"*How* would I want to be treated if I were in their situation?"

If I ponder this long enough, my truthful answer tells me how to handle the situation, because after all, I want to be treated well, fair, and right! I know I am not perfect and do things wrong at times, so if I am supposed to be treated with discipline, that's fine too. I will learn through the discipline if it is done in love. I want to be treated with honesty, dignity, kindness, respect, compassion, love, forgiveness, mercy, and so on. Okay, but knowing how I want to be treated still makes the answer easier said than done sometimes. A common saying that is interconnected with the golden rule says to put myself in another's shoes, and then I will know what to do. I know from experience that this can literally change everything. Living the golden rule is supposed to be my way of life. Jesus says this is the way it is to be done. It is spiritual. Many times the only way to know what to do is to ask God what to do. He has the whole picture. It is a challenging, growing experience that is worth striving for. Every circumstance is different, and each one of them requires the Holy Spirit's perfect knowledge on how to handle each and every situation. God the father, Jesus the Son, and the Holy Spirit all agree on how it should be done. Of course, it is never done, meaning finished. I can't just say, "Well, I've been there and done that, and it is over," because it is never over in this lifetime. There will always be new challenges to test and strengthen this way of life. This is a lifestyle, the Christian lifestyle that the Holy Trinity helps us learn how to do.

I admit that I have had difficult times with this before, and I have failed in it before, but never, never ever have I had an experience that equals the one I am going to tell you about. I have never had to use the golden rule in the midst of shock, in the midst of pain and agony, but I know *someone* … oh, yes I do … I know someone who did.

I met her on the phone on what was the worst day of my life, and it was the worst day of her life. It was on this worst of all days that death became my teacher about the golden rule. Death had lots to teach me, and I had nowhere to run from it and nowhere to hide. I found out I hadn't even begun to explore the golden rule, and most of the time, I had even taken it for granted, not fully realizing the extent of its power.

Oh, yes, the golden rule has immense power.

Death became a teacher to me when I was stripped bare of life as I knew it. It was a teacher like no other, because I was forced to look at eternity as a reality. Eternity had always been in the future, and that is where I wanted it! Now it had entered my present.

Our child had left our earthly home, never physically to come back, call, or visit. When I was forced to enter into this new life, created by death, life became richer, deeper, and more meaningful, mixed together with the pain and the agony. This is the time when I learned why the golden rule is called golden. No other time in my life had it ever glowed as brilliantly as it did during the blackest hour of despair. I was on the receiving end of such a gift, and I knew it was the purest, most perfect gift I had ever received in my entire life from another human being.

I had cried out from the depths of my soul, "No, no, no, no, no." I couldn't quit saying no.

I was bent double with pain and anguish.

The sword that was thrust into my heart all the way down into my soul took a sudden new gut-wrenching twist. We received the rest of the horrible news that morning of May 19, 1996.

Jeremy was not by himself in the car. A girl, a beautiful young girl, was also killed in the accident. Amanda had been in the front seat of the car with him. Jeremy and Amanda both died instantly. Joe, the friend Jeremy was going to spend the night with, was in intensive care in the hospital.

This was too much. This was too hard to bear. This simply couldn't be happening. I could not stand it. I just couldn't understand how this could all be true, but they told me it was true. It was the longest day of my life. Time just plain stopped for me. People were everywhere in our house and outside our house. I really didn't know where I was. It was a different world from the one I had always known, and I didn't know where I fit. Actually, I knew I didn't fit. I didn't fit anywhere. I was suspended in an unknown world all by myself even though there were people all around us taking care of us in this new world that had been created since the accident.

Our minister, Scott, had called us at 5: a.m. and told Billy about Jeremy's death, and it was exactly twelve hours later, at 5:00 p.m. when another call came. This is the call I am talking about. A lady I didn't know wanted to speak to us. They told me it was Rosemary, Amanda's mother.

I cried, "How could I talk to Amanda's mother? What could I possibly say?"

I knew there were no words that were adequate. My sorrow of her daughter's death was not enough to give her. I thought I would die of unspeakable pain. I took the phone with trembling hands, not knowing what would happen. I had no idea that this was an extraordinary woman. She made the first step toward us.

I said, "Hello," and she spoke the most loving words possible. She wanted us to know that they did not blame our son or us for what had happened. She expressed to me that she could put herself in our shoes, because ... *they also had a teenage son named Jeremy. This could have happened to him too.*

I felt like falling to the floor on my knees, weeping with so much grief, weeping with thankfulness for her reaching out to us, weeping because of her kindness and compassion for us that she had in the midst of her very own grief. I cry, even now, as I write these beautiful words. I stop writing, and I cry. No, I weep, because weeping is bigger, deeper than crying. Weeping goes all the way to my core. I weep because I am still overwhelmed with gratitude and thankfulness for the golden gift that she gave.

She was merciful. She was forgiving. She was love. And it was during the time that her own world had fallen apart and she was heartbroken. Her soul had been pierced too. The sword of death was all the way through her. Yet she thought of us and our anguish.

All of these gifts that she bestowed on us were not of this world. No, they weren't. These gifts came from the Father. They were spiritual gifts that were more valuable than earthly treasures and still are because they were gifts that live beyond the grave. They are gifts for the here and now and also gifts that are laid up as treasures in heaven. They belong to her eternal inheritance.

In Matthew 6:19–21 (NIV) Jesus said, "Do not store up for yourselves treasures on earth, where moth and rust destroy, and where thieves break in and steal. But store up for yourselves treasures in heaven, where moth and rust do not destroy, and where thieves do not break in and steal. For where your treasure is, there your heart will be also."

I will take every one of these treasures that she gave me ... kindness, mercy, forgiveness, compassion, and love ... with me when I go to heaven. They abide in my heart. They are precious jewels living inside of me, and I will show them to the Father. I will thank Him for loving me through His precious Rosemary whom He loves with all His heart because He knows her heart belongs to Him. How blessed is the love of God that we can give to one another! When I go to heaven, I will leave all my physical treasures down here for someone else to own for a while until their time is up, but these living, eternal gifts in my heart will go with me to heaven and be with me forever, and they will live forever.

Mercy, forgiveness, compassion, and love cannot be bought or sold, and we can't make someone give them to us either. They can only be given freely. Rosemary extended the utmost forgiveness at the time most needed. She portrayed a life of faith, a life of love and compassion. She had compassion for us that helped me bear something that was beyond my own ability to bear.

Even in her grief, she helped hold me up in my hour of agony.

All of these gifts were wrapped up inside that golden rule that lives in her heart. She unwrapped the gifts, and then she reached out to us and gave them away.

I feel in my heart that Amanda and Jeremy were together witnessing this heavenly gesture that was given from one heartbroken mother to another heartbroken mother. I know they were right in the middle of it. It was a moment that brought heaven and earth together as one, and I feel that Jeremy and Amanda held on to each other in this moment of purity and love. And I believe the angels wept with joy. The angels are joyful when God's will is done.

The golden rule is truly golden. It comes from that golden city of heaven. Christ the King holds it out to us from inside us where He lives. He plants it in our hearts to be used when needed. And He allows us to be the ones to put it to use and to give it way. It doesn't glisten to others without our permission. We have the freedom to use it if we are willing. It has to be brought forth from inside us, by us to bestow on others. We are rich indeed to have such gold inside of us to dig out and bring forth.

When we activate the golden rule, it has great power to give strength to the spirits of others.

The Lord greatly blesses you, Rosemary, for who you are and the gift that you gave to us. I will never ever forget you. You became a light that shone in our darkness of despair and will always shine for me for the rest of my life. It not only shines on earth, it sparkles and shimmers in heaven, and the angels rejoice over you. You are the full, complete expression of Christianity.

> So in everything, do to others
> what you would have them do to you,
> for this sums up the Law and the Prophets.
> —Matthew 7:12 (NIV)

LOVE BEYOND MEASURE

It seemed the day that Jeremy died would have no end to it. The sword had plunged into my heart, twisted when I learned Joe was in intensive care, then gouged even deeper when I learned of Amanda's death, and then jabbed as deep as possible by more news. Jeremy was being used as an example. I could not believe what I was hearing. What was to come was a nightmare in itself. We had no clue that his death would trigger an enormous issue in our county and become a heated debate in the newspaper. We were blasted again when we found out that he became The Example immediately following his death.

We were learning bits and pieces of the night before. Here is what happened:

Jeremy attended a field party located at a ballpark in our county. There had been over seven hundred in attendance, which included mostly teens and not enough chaperones. At 2:00 a.m., Jeremy and his two friends were invited to go to another friend's home that was close by. His friend's father had volunteered to fix breakfast for them. They had traveled a few miles and were about half a mile from the friend's house when the accident happened. Yes, that's right ... only half a mile.

The police reported that alcohol and speed contributed to the accident. Jeremy was the driver of the car. Immediately, controversy over the field party event was charged like an electric current. We were not aware of the field party, and neither were the police or a lot of other parents. There was anger, fear, and regret mixed in with the grief that was enveloping the county. There was talk of putting Jeremy's wrecked car on display either at the county courthouse or in front of the high school for all to see. This was to be used as an example to other teens to make them think about the consequences of drinking and driving.

The very thought of this caused sickening pain inside me.

My thoughts were screaming, *No, no, no! If our son's death is not enough, you cannot have his car!*

I am being honest. This is how I felt. Why should our son be used as an example? Why should our son's car be put on display?

I wanted to scream, "Your children came home; our child did *not*. Isn't that enough?"

I didn't say any of these thoughts. I just said one word. "No!"

People were shocked at my answer. This was not like the Rhonda they had known all of their lives. Well, you see, I wasn't that same Rhonda and never would be again. That sword of death had wounded me, and the wound was fresh. It felt like it was bleeding profusely.

I was asked, "Don't you want good to come out of this horrible tragedy?"

Well, quite frankly, at the time ... I didn't care!

My heart was cut so deep that I could barely breathe. It was painfully raw, and it felt like it was bleeding inside. I felt stripped of everything. I felt as though there was nothing inside of me, and I had nothing to give. I was running on zero. I was empty and had nothing to offer.

We are complex creatures. I was split inside over this. In my mind, I totally understood the reasoning of displaying the car. I understood it completely. This horrible tragedy had been a shock to the entire county, and it was a wake-up call to do something to help protect our teens. And yes, perhaps this could be a beneficial thing for others to view this mangled car. I understood all of this.

If it had not been my child who was dead, I might have thought this would be a very good thing to do. I knew there was a tremendous lesson learned here, not only for teens but for adults as well. I knew that. However, I had never been on this end of a request like this before; I was in a different place.

I thought about giving into the request, but ... but ... but ... I couldn't.

I went to the Lord in prayer. It was more than I could bear on my own. "Help me, Lord," I cried.

My heart was shattered. My heart was so injured and sick that I couldn't bear the thought of it. It was my soul, my very being that wanted to protect my son's dignity in his death. My mind, my heart, and my soul could not agree on this matter, and it sickened me.

My teacher, death, was not finished with me. I was to learn more truth about myself than I had ever known before because I was put to this test. I would have never dreamed that I would have reacted this way, because I am truly a giver by nature. Sometimes, I am even too much of a giver for my own good.

I questioned my intense reaction of absolute revulsion to the request of putting his car on display. After all, it was only a car.

However, to me, there was more to it than that. It was my baby's car, and he had died in it. I doubled over in grief. He had loved that car. He was always working on it, washing, polishing, shining it inside and out. It ripped me apart to think it would be displayed as an example of what could happen as a result of field parties. To me, it seemed unfair and unreasonable (even though I understood it in my mind) for us to carry this heavy, heavy load for everybody else. I couldn't even hold myself up. The burden was far too heavy, and I just couldn't do it.

It was on the day that my son died that I realized my true self could not (absolutely could not) willingly give my child for anybody. I could give my life for my child's life, but I could never, ever, ever give my child's life for anybody or anything. He could have offered his life, but I couldn't have offered it.

Then my mind cried out, "What about Abraham?"

(Abraham? What's he got to do with this?)

"God, what are you talking about, and what am I supposed to learn here?"

It's amazing how God speaks to us internally and through His Word. He brought this to my mind to help me sort out what was going on in my mind and emotions. It was my job to talk to the Lord about this and get some peace of mind.

Well, I knew that Abraham was willing to sacrifice his son to God, and

I couldn't even give my own son's car as a symbol of what can happen as a result of field parties and in the hope that it could save lives in the future.

I wrestled with feelings of guilt and unworthiness until I realized that God had asked Abraham to do this. God had not asked me to do anything. Other people were asking me, but God wasn't asking me.

I turned to Genesis, chapter 22 and read about God testing Abraham's faith and obedience to Him. As I studied Abraham's willingness to do what God had asked him to do, which was to slay his son, Isaac, as a burnt sacrifice to Him, I also understood that Abraham fully expected, 100 percent believed (faith) that God would take care of Isaac's life somehow and some way during this. He knew they both would come back down from that mountain! This is what Abraham told his servants. He said for them to wait for them while He and Isaac went on further to worship God and that after that, they, Abraham *and* Isaac, would be back. Abraham remembered God's covenant with him and God saying that this covenant would last forever! He believed God when He said that Isaac was to be the one who was ordained in this covenant. Isaac was to be the one to carry the ancestry of many kings of the Jews continuing until the greatest king, the Messiah, would come! These were to be the ancestors of Jesus Christ, and they are found in the first chapter of Matthew of the New Testament. Abraham and Isaac are the first two mentioned! It all starts with them (both of them)! There was complete trust and faith from Abraham's mind, heart, and soul that God would take care of Isaac that day on that mountain, and Abraham was right! God did take care of the situation.

God stopped Abraham from slaying Isaac as a sacrifice to Him, and He even provided the ram for Abraham to sacrifice instead of his son. Abraham knew all along that somehow, someway, God would provide the sacrifice, because that is what he told Isaac when he was tying him up! Abraham passed his test, proving that he loved God first in his life and was willing to obey and trust Him even with his own son, Isaac.

God knew what Abraham would be willing to do, but it was not necessary for him to do it. God had His own plan all along, and it was to come from Abraham's descendants, fulfilled when He sent the Lamb of God, His one and only Son, to be the ultimate sacrifice. God's plan was to sacrifice *His* own Son. There is only one symbol that represents the saving of lives ... and that symbol is the cross.

Road Trip: Jesus, Jeremy and Me

I stayed in the bed most of that day because I couldn't even stay up. I would get up and walk around the house and then go right back to bed. I did not have the strength, the heart, or spirit to stay up. People were all around my bed. I knew they were there, but it was one big blur.

My mind traveled back to the prayers that were prayed early that morning. I was the last one to pray, and I remembered thanking God for giving us such a sweet little baby boy to love and cherish for seventeen years and to please help us through the grief of not having him with us anymore. I thought about that prayer, and suddenly memories of him as a baby surged through my brain like a hot, searing iron. A hot, searing iron burns and can leave bad blisters. These memories were like that, because even though they were wonderful memories, now they were hot and burning with pain, because he wasn't here anymore. As I remembered vividly the preparations we made while we waited for his arrival, his birth and his death seemed all wrapped together as one big bundle.

I doubled over in pain. "Oh my! Dear God, how ... *how* ... in the world did You do it? How did You give your Son for us? I can't even give my son's wrecked car to be put on display." I was lying in bed, but I fell to my knees in my mind, doubled over in pain.

For various reasons, the car issue was dropped. God in His mercy took care of the situation. The fact was there was no need to put the car on display. Kids flocked to where the car was parked. They went because they *wanted* to. It wasn't on display to teach them a lesson. They went to the car instead of the car glaring at them as an ugly reminder. They went out of love, and they came to us and told us about it. They shared their feelings and broken hearts with us, and we cried together. The car became a meeting place, not because of a mangled car but because of the love they held in their hearts for the boy who had driven the car.

We never saw the wrecked car. We only remembered it as it was when Jeremy loved and enjoyed it.

As time passed, we saw the tremendously good things that came out of our tragedy. There were many. Lots of lives were changed, but it was God who made good come out of bad. It didn't come from our sacrifice, because we didn't give it. We simply don't have that kind of power. I learned more about my frailties and weaknesses when my only son died. Lives were changed because of God working in it and through it. All glory, praise, and honor go the Father who loves us beyond measure.

I have an even greater understanding of what God did for us. There is no greater sacrifice than to willingly give your child so that others might live. God gave the ultimate sacrifice. I knew it in my mind, but now I actually felt it from the depths of my soul, and I am humbled. I am blessed, and I am thankful. I learned that I cannot fathom such love as this. It is hard to comprehend, and it simply cannot be measured.

Oh, how the apostle Paul wants us to ponder this great love that God has for us. He wants us to feel it from the top of our heads to the bottom of our feet. He wants us to let it flow through us and all around us. He wants us to let this great love saturate our souls.

Paul says that when he thinks of God's wisdom and the scope of His almighty plan, he falls on his knees and prays to the Father. He prays to the Father of all of us, and His being the Father of all of us means the ones who are already in heaven and the rest of us who are still down here on earth. He talks about our roots. He prays that our roots go down deep into God's love and that we may be able to feel and understand how long, how wide, how deep His love really is. He prays that we can experience this love for ourselves and know that even though it is so great, we will never see the end of it or fully know or understand it; we will be filled up with it (Ephesians 3: 14–19)!

There are no earthly words that can describe how big this love is. There are words that describe big, such as great, enormous, huge, vast, immense, and gigantic, to name a few, but they do not even begin to name it, because there is no end to this love. It is like eternity where there is no measurement. There is no measurement for God's definitions of long, wide, or deep.

I failed the earthly test in my heart to give to other people. I was drained. I was too empty to give more, but I knew that God loved me anyway. I know that God made us to have a longing to be held when we need comforting. We are like Him. He wants to hold us too.

God opened up His arms. I crawled up in His lap. He rocked me gently in my grief, and I felt the gift of love beyond measure.

GOD'S BABY BOOK

As God rocked me in His lap, wonderful, warm peace began to steal over me. I felt loved and cherished and safe. I thought more about my baby and God's baby. When my baby died, my eyes were opened wide to see more clearly what God did when He came to earth.

I contemplated it and still do at times. The worst happened to me in 1996, and the best happened to me. I carry it with me like a purse full of treasures. Without the worst, I wouldn't have had the best. Without the best, I wouldn't have had the worst. The worst was the death of my precious Jeremy, and the best was God coming to me. The best was having Jeremy for seventeen earthly years, and the worst was being separated by death.

Those memories of Jeremy as a baby kept coming and wouldn't let up. I was remembering vividly all those wonderful preparations we made while we waited for his arrival. I anticipated the doctor visits to make sure everything was proceeding as it should. We fixed his room, using the same baby bed that Julie had slept in. We were so proud of that room. And little Julie was too. She was close to four years old. Julie's birthday is July 7, and Jeremy's birthday is July 11. They were close to being exactly four years apart. She played with his new clothes, gifts, bottles, and everything we needed for him. She was looking forward to the baby's arrival. All was in order. We waited for his birth.

Jeremy had just been gone for a few hours when his birth and his death seemed to be wrapped up all together as one event, and all of it was so painful because he was gone. The pain was so great, and I wanted my baby back.

I wanted my baby back! I wanted to hold my baby. It was then that I thought of God's grief of His Son's death. God was talking to me, understanding my pain. It was then that my Savior's birth and death began to merge together within me as well! I stopped crying. I listened. I was being told something. He started reminding me how He had planned for His baby to come to earth! Yes, He had. He had planned too! We are like our Father in heaven! Oh how wonderful! He showed me how He had planned perfectly for His Son's birth even down to His birth announcements!

My eyes were opened to the fact of how the family tree of Jesus was of monumental importance to God. He started preparing for his baby's arrival on earth not for nine months as we do but for thousands of years before His birth! God chose everything.

God chose Abraham to be the one to start the genealogy of Jesus. God spoke (There is that word again!) to Abraham. He told him that all peoples on earth would be blessed through him, through his seed. Abraham was very dear to God's heart, and He chose Abraham to be His Son's ancestor. He spoke a promise to Abraham, and Abraham believed God. Abraham and Sarah had to wait years for their baby to come, but Abraham believed it would happen. It was an absolute miracle that they were able to have their son, Isaac, because they were so old … but that is how God works. He is the miracle maker. He is mysterious.

The family tree of Jesus continued from Abraham with the birth of Isaac. Then God started predicting the coming of His Son throughout the Old Testament, using His beloved prophets to proclaim that the Messiah was indeed coming. The King is coming. This Messiah would establish a kingdom that would never end.

God's chosen people, descendants of Abraham and Sarah, were as numerous as the stars, just as He had promised Abraham and Sarah that they would be. The prophets were given details of the divine birth that was to come, of the divine kingdom that would be established. It was foretold that the Messiah would be born in Bethlehem, born of a virgin of all things! God chose the mother of His Son and sent a message to her directly from Him. An angel told her exactly what was going to happen

ROAD TRIP: JESUS, JEREMY AND ME

and how she would become the mother of the Messiah, the Son of the Living God. Her name was Mary.

The complete genealogy of Jesus is the first thing to be recorded in the New Testament. The time had finally come. It was the precise time, the right time.

God sent out personal announcements about His baby boy being born. Oh, yes, He did! He sent angels singing in the sky. Angels announced His baby's birth! There has never been a birth announcement like this. It was one of a kind! I cannot imagine that glorious scene in the sky and the music they sang. It was a baby announcement never to be forgotten.

The sky told of His birth with a special star leading the wise men who came from a faraway place.

God's creation was involved in this wondrous event of His baby's birth.

What planning! What love for His one and only begotten Son! What love for us, His adopted children!

All this information is found in the most amazing, fascinating, astonishing, and truthful baby book that I know. I held it in my hands and just kept looking at it.

It is the Holy Bible!

The Holy Bible is Jesus's baby book!

Why had I never seen this truth before? Not only that ... it is our baby book too. It tells us where we came from, how we got here, why we are here, how we are connected to the Father of the universe, how we are supposed to act, what we are supposed to do while we are here, how we are connected to our brother Jesus and what He is like, and where we go when we leave here! We have the entire scope of our existence in this book.

I cried. Oh, yes, I did. I wept. The Word of God was more real to me than it had ever been, because I could *feel* the pain of the Father, even in the joyous preparations he was making of His Son coming to earth. He knew every detail that was ahead for His Son, even knew the cruel way he would die. I cried, I wept for my Jeremy. I still wanted him back; this did not change my pain. There is pain in breaking the family circle down here on earth. God knows all about that pain. He endured it too when His Son died. He knew Mary's pain and grief of losing her son. He knew the pain of His Son's disciples and other followers. He knew the pain His Son had endured. But God held on to His commitment to Abraham and to all people on earth. He carried everybody's pain! He went through it anyway. None of this new information took away my physical pain of separation, but it connected me to the lifeline of heavenly creation that understood what I was going through and knew my pain, every bit of it.

We prepare for our babies to come to earth. We send out joyful announcements. We make baby books. We are like our heavenly Father. He did the same things. We are made in His image. What a glorious Father we have!

PSALM 139

I had to get out of bed. I didn't want to, but I had to. I had to get dressed so we could go to the funeral home. We had to talk to Field, the funeral director. He was a dear friend whom we had known all of our lives. He was close in age to us. One of his daughters, Katie, was in Jeremy's graduation class. Katie was heartbroken. Field was heartbroken, and his kindness knew no bounds. He gently helped and guided us in making the decisions that had to be made. We had to pick out a casket, choose a vault, and decide what times we wanted visitation and when we wanted to schedule the funeral.

I came home numb. I remember going into my office and sitting down at my desk. I didn't know what else to do. I was still somewhat in shock, still trying to absorb all these changes. We had to plan a funeral. That was all there was to it. I knew we couldn't do this by ourselves without the Lord's help.

I picked up my Bible, held it in my hands, and opened it up. Holding the Bible or having it close by me gave me comfort. I laid it on my desk and stared at it, not knowing what pages to turn. I had no idea where I wanted to go in it. I looked at where I had opened my Bible, and my eyes fell on the most beautiful words. I knew that God was speaking to me. King David is talking to the Lord, acknowledging His great power and His wonderful love. It was Psalm, chapter 139.

All of a sudden, I was snapped to attention because the words I was reading came *alive*! I read the first few verses, and it was if God was speaking directly to me. I heard Him speak my name as I was reading His words. It was so wonderful because I was not in good shape. I needed to hear from my heavenly Father. The precious Holy Spirit spoke gently to my aching heart:

"Rhonda, I know you inside and out because I have examined your heart. I know everything about you. I know every time you sit down and every time you stand up. I know your every thought. I know where you are every moment of every day, and I will guide you and tell you where to go and when to stop, if you will let me. I know what you are going to say before you even say it. I am in front of you, and I am behind you."

I sat back in my chair in wonder. Wow, wow, wow! I knew then that God had guided me to this very spot by His Holy Spirit, who lives in me. He was talking directly to me!

I read on about what King David had to say about these glorious, truthful things that He had just written to the Lord. He was writing these things about God toward himself, because He knew this was the way it was. (Still is!) Here is what King David said in his words: "O Lord, you have searched me and you know me. You know when I sit and when I rise; you perceive my thoughts from afar. You discern my going out and my lying down; you are familiar with all my ways. Before a word is on my tongue you know it completely, Oh Lord. You hem me in—behind and before; you have laid your hand upon me. Such knowledge is too wonderful for me, too lofty for me to attain" (Psalm 139:1–6 NIV).

King David exclaimed that this was so glorious and so wonderful that it was hard to believe these things! He realized that he could never be lost to the Spirit of God. He could never get away to anywhere and be away from God! No matter where he went, God's hand would guide him, and God's strength would support him.

God speaks all these wonderful things to all of us, His children. It just wasn't for King David. He knows all if us inside out whether we acknowledge it or not. There is not one thing He doesn't know. He is all knowing. He loves us so much that He is with us constantly. I wondered why we don't memorize this chapter 139 like we do the twenty-third psalm. This chapter should be imprinted in our minds, hearts, and souls also. What healing, majestic words to have in my mind! He knew I needed His comfort, His strength, His guidance, His love for me and also in

ROAD TRIP: JESUS, JEREMY AND ME

picking out scripture to be read at Jeremy's funeral. There it was ... all of it in that one chapter. Oh, what a chapter! It was in the next verses that I found exactly what I was looking for to be read at Jeremy's funeral. I personalized it too as I read it. This is what I heard.

("God, you made all of Jeremy's delicate, inner parts of his body and knit them together in my womb. Thank you, Lord, for making him so wonderful and so complete. It amazes me to even think about Jeremy's wonderfulness. You were there with him while he was being formed. He was not alone in me; you were there with him. You saw him before he was born here on earth, and you scheduled each day of his life before he even began to breathe. Every day of his life was recorded in your book!")

Oh, my, my, my! Is that powerful or what?

Here is the way it is written in the Bible: "For you created my inmost being; you knit me together in my mother's womb. I praise you because I am fearfully and wonderfully made; your works are wonderful, I know that full well. My frame was not hidden from you when I was made in the secret place. When I was woven together in the depths of the earth, your eyes saw my unformed body. All the days ordained for me were written in your book before one of them came to be" (Psalm 139:13–16 NIV).

Jeremy was never ever alone. God knew him before he was born, never left his side while his physical body was being formed, knew exactly how long he would be on earth, and even wrote down everything about each and every day of his life. He knew his heart, knew every time he sat down, knew every time he got up, knew every thought he ever had and was with him every moment of his life. And He is still with him!

I clutched my Bible to my chest, and I cried. I cried tears of joy and tears of sorrow all mixed together. God is faithful. God is love. He gave me what I needed at the precise time I needed it.

The lives of all God's children are that precious to Him. He is all knowing, all-powerful, and always present. Wherever we are ... God is there too.

> I praise you because I am fearfully and wonderfully made;
> Your works are wonderful,
> I know that full well.
>
> —Psalm 139:14 (NIV)

GOD IS STILL IN CONTROL

Graduation was in two weeks. Jeremy was so close to finishing, completing twelve years of his education. We had come this far in our life's journey with him, and this was going to be one of his big steps toward manhood. I gazed at the invitations that had not been mailed out, and I looked at the cap and gown. You know what they meant to me now? They meant nothing except pain. They represented what almost happened. They were already things of the past instead of the anticipation of what was to come. They were absolutely empty and useless vessels.

I remembered how good it had felt when Julie graduated from high school. Of course, it was an emotional mix of letting go to get ready for what was next in her life. On her graduation night, I had felt such an overwhelming feeling of pride for her accomplishments, and I was looking forward to this same wonderful feeling of coming to this new threshold in Jeremy's life, but now everything had changed.

What do you do when you have to plan a funeral instead of a party? You do it. It is as simple as that. You just do it. I look back, and I am amazed at the fact that we could make the decisions that needed to be made. I do remember what the driving force was that propelled us forward with this. It was the fact that this would be the last physical thing that we would ever do for our son. The very last physical thing we could ever do. I will have to say that the shock and numbness that accompanied our grief was a blessing that helped us move through all the motions of decision

ROAD TRIP: JESUS, JEREMY AND ME

making. Julie became our rock that we leaned on. It was as if she took on the parent role. Together we seemed instinctively to know how to pull it all together.

So much had happened in so little time. So much had changed. I had never felt such pain in my life. The next day, I was driven, and I mean driven to the Bible to read the book of Job. Have you ever felt driven to do something? It was if it had hold on me. I know that this feeling of being driven toward Job was from the Holy Spirit. I clutched the Bible to my chest, hugging it close, wanting it to hold me in my pain. I knew the Word of God was powerful beyond words, beyond the physical, beyond what we can see. I knew it was the Holy Spirit who was propelling me forward to meet Job in his pain. The Holy Spirit is the Comforter, and He knew where I could get the utmost comfort at that time. He knew that I knew Job's story, but now I knew a part of Job's pain. Knowing what happened to Job was one thing, but being able to feel some of what he felt gave me an added dimension of kinship with him that I never knew before. The Holy Spirit wanted me to meet the man named Job and know him in a personal way, which goes beyond knowing his story.

When I finished reading Job, I loved him. Oh, yes, I did. When I get to heaven, I want to wrap my arms around Job. He is my kinfolk now. I want to sit with him and acknowledge the pain he suffered on earth. I want to commend him on his great, unwavering faith in God, and I want to listen to what he has to say. I am very much looking forward to this visit with such a wonderful person who never gave up on God. Job had ten times my pain because he had ten children die all at the same time. I cannot begin to imagine the pain he suffered, yet I felt so related to Job. It was on a small scale comparing my suffering to his suffering, but even so, I felt very close to him, and I wanted his comfort. I knew he could comfort me. I knew Job knew my pain. I read his whole book. It did comfort me very much because the Holy Bible is alive and real and has the power to comfort. I knew, I just knew, if Job could survive all of his tragedies, then I could survive mine.

I learned something I didn't know before. I really *like* Job. I like what he stood for, and I liked reading about him. I liked his courage and his realness as a person. He was so honest with his feelings. It made me want to be like him. I liked the fact that Job was a very spiritual man who loved God totally. He was a good man, generous to others, law abiding, respectful, and respected. I admire all of these qualities that made up Job's character and personality. It was evident from his actions that he loved his children very much. He was a great family man and head of his household in a good positive way. He didn't put the responsibility of parenthood totally on his wife's shoulders, because he joined her in it, becoming a team in taking care of their children. He gave himself to his children. He was proud of them. He had seven sons and three daughters. His children were very close to each other. His sons would take turns holding feasts in their homes and invite their three sisters. Job waited for these feasts to run their course, and after these feasts, Job would get his children together, all ten of them. He would then sanctify them and offer a burnt offering for each one of them. He loved them so much that he wanted to make sure they hadn't sinned and turned away from God in their hearts. Wow! What a father! What love he had for his children and for God! How could they not feel love from their father? Even though Job was a very wealthy man, he wanted his children to know humbleness, reverence, and awe for God. I am humbled myself just reading about it. The sincerity and faith of this sweet man is such an example of wonderful fatherhood. This was at the top of his list of priorities! His first thought was to make sure his children were okay with God and to remind them that God comes first. This was true love! He knew that this life was temporary, and the main thing was to stay focused on the life to come with God Almighty. In my opinion, Job was a giant in love and leadership.

Everything was going so well in Job's life when all of a sudden everything was wiped away. Life came to a sudden, jerking, jolting stop. Why? The answer is in the power of spoken words.

Yes, the devil came to face God, and with words from his mouth, he started dripping his poison. He couldn't stand the fact that Job was so faithful and wonderful and blessed by God. You see, Satan wanted Job! Satan is so greedy. He absolutely couldn't stand the fact that Job would have nothing to do with him and his evil ways. The nasty things he said about Job and his character make me so angry. He is such a liar! He enjoys testing God's people. He is that nasty.

He predicted that if God took away Job's blessings that Job would not be the same man. He insinuated that because God had provided Job with protection from harm in every way and given him wealth and prosperity, that it was easy for Job to worship God. This really makes no sense to me because sometimes when we have everything, we tend to forget about God! This made Job even more special, because he didn't take anything for granted. However, the devil didn't want to give Job credit for that! He doesn't give anybody credit for anything! He is strictly a liar and manipulator at all times. He couldn't wait to test Job to the limit.

Well, since God is God, He knows the outcome of everything. He knew Job's motives came from his pure, sincere heart. He knows truth, and He knows the devil is a liar. However, He allowed the devil to test Job's character and his love for God. You see, God was not troubled by this. He knew Job would be in horrible pain, but it would be temporary. He would always and forever take care of Job. God knew how Job would become a universal comfort to all of us through his endurance of suffering. He knew Job would gain victory that was his at the end of it all.

The devil, Satan, began his evil work immediately. He does have lots of power, and it is in his nature to do evil; therefore, He couldn't wait to attack. He instigated the Sabeans to raid Job's property in a terrible way. They ran his oxen away, and that was a lot because he had five hundred of them. They also ran off his five hundred female donkeys and then killed all of Job's farmhands. Oh no! That is just terrible! He then rained down fire, burning up all seven thousand of Job's sheep and their herdsmen. Oh no! That is horrible!

He continued by entering the hearts of the Chaldeans to drive off all of Job's camels and kill all of the servants that were with them. Oh no, no, no! All of this is so brutal!

Job's wealth was now gone.

Then he did the ultimate when He found all of Job's sons and daughters eating together at their oldest brother's home. He sent a mighty wind that tore up the house, causing it to fall in. Everyone there was killed. This killed every one of Job's precious children.

All of this happened on the same day, with messengers continually running to Job with all the terrible news. He had already heard about losing all of his wealth when he got the message about his children. It was hearing about his children that brought him to his knees. When he heard of his children's deaths, he stood up, tore his robe in grief, and fell to the ground. Job said that God had given him everything that he had, and it was all His to take away. Even in his grief, he acknowledged that his children belonged to the Lord, and they were His to take away. He knew his children were with the Lord even then at that very moment! He worshipped God in his grief and did not sin.

Job lost everything in a matter of hours—his wealth, his servants, and his children, but the devil was still not satisfied, so he struck Job's health. Job had a terrible case of boils from his head to his toes, and he sat in ashes, scraping his skin with a broken piece of pottery. His wife tried to get him to curse God and die, but Job would not. He looked so awful from all of this that he even said himself that he was scary to look at. However, in all of this, Job still did not give up on God. He wanted one thing. All he wanted was to die and get out of the agonizing torture and pain.

His friends came to comfort him. Job had changed so much they didn't even recognize him! It hit them hard. They wailed in sorrow for Job, and they comforted him for seven days. How did they comfort him? They just sat with him in his pain, which was the best thing they could have ever done. It was just what Job needed to support him in his misery.

The only trouble was that after seven days, they started talking. If they had only kept their mouths shut! It was spoken words that became the last straw that finished breaking him down. After seven days of silence, Job started pouring out his heart to them, his agony and his sorrow. It was exactly what he needed to do! To help start releasing the pain from his body, to start pouring it out could have been the start of healing for Job. There was just one problem. They couldn't handle his sorrow. The devil even had the nerve to step into Job's grief, making sure that his friends would not understand him or bring comfort to him in his grief. Instead of just letting Job vent his pain and his sorrow, they turned on him! Yes, they did. They started condemning, judging, and scoffing at him. They spoke poison from their lips. It was cruel and condemning, and from their speaking, they created more grief and burdens for Job to carry! Job absolutely wanted to die.

He continued to pour out his tears to God. His hopes were gone, his heart's desires were broken, his friends didn't believe in him anymore, and not only that, they were being downright cruel to him. Job asked his friends just how long were they going to work (the devil's work) at breaking his spirit down completely with their words. His body was already broken down, and now they were breaking down his spirit. It was so bad that he even asked them why they weren't ashamed of themselves for dealing with him so harshly when he was already suffering so much that he wanted to die. Well, Satan is just that—cruel. He worked through the men's egos so much that all they cared about was being right and telling Job what they thought about all of this. They had the nerve to think they knew why Job was suffering at this magnitude.

I cannot even imagine the suffering of this great soul. It was if he had nothing pertaining to this life left. They tried to convince him that he had done something wrong and evil for all of this to have happened in his life. They tried to shove guilt down his throat and wanted him to swallow it. Job was down as far as he could get, and then the devil used his friends to kick him and beat him with their words. Job didn't know of anything he had done that could have caused all this to happen to him. His friends did not believe him, and they rallied against him to tell the truth. What kind of friends were these? They had become his worst enemies. They were self-righteous, condemning, arrogant, and judgmental.

Through all of this, Job still believed in God and never gave up. He felt like dying and wanted to die, but he held on. He still believed that when he died, he would see God. He was convinced of that fact. Nothing was going to change his mind.

Reading about Job's strength gave me strength. Reading about his strength and courage gave me strength, courage, and comfort. It was spiritual medicine being poured over my suffering soul, and believe me, I soaked it in.

I marveled at how Job hung on and wouldn't let go. If he could survive all of this torment, I knew that I could survive. If Job could continue to have faith, so could I. I could relate to Job. I was having a piece of his suffering. Job was human, as am I. He felt like dying, his pain was so great, yet he knew this one thing, and he held on to it with all his might:

God was still in control.

This was the greatest medicine of all for me. I somehow knew if I hung on to the fact that God was still in control of His creations of earth, the universe, and everything in it, I would be okay, that everything would be okay.

God knew how strong Job's faith was, and He knew how much suffering Job could stand without breaking. He never left Job but watched and listened the whole time. He let Job vent, talk it out with his friends, and he let his friends voice their opinions and judgments. He listened as Job asked the big question of "Why, why, why?" Job wanted an explanation from God to ease his pain. It is in our human nature to ask "Why?" when grief hits. Don't ever think you are the only person in the world that ever asks this monumental question of "Why?"! It is a normal human response to suffering.

After much struggle and grief, God did answer Job. He came in a whirlwind and spoke from it. He told Job He did not owe anyone anything. He is God. He did not owe Job an explanation. The important thing was that Job was faithful through all of it, but God was very angry at Job's three friends for the way they had treated Job in his grief. He said they had not been right about what they said about Him and what they had said about Job. He told the three men what to do to get forgiveness from Him. They had a job to do, give burnt sacrifices to God, and Job had a job to do, pray for them! God said that he would accept Job's prayer on their behalf and would not destroy them as He should because of the way they had treated Job. Now, how about that? After Job's friends had been so nasty to him, God wanted Job to pray for them! Oh my, my, my! Wonder how Job felt about *that*? In the end, God knew that Job needed to forgive the men too so that he could go on with his life and not carry the baggage of un-forgiveness.

God blessed Job at the end of his life even more than He had when all of this began. His wealth was doubled in size, and he had ten more children. It says that his three daughters were the most beautiful girls in the land. He lived another 140 years after that and knew his grandchildren and great-grandchildren.

What truly mattered in all of this was the confident assurance that God was still in control. Only He sees and knows the big picture in its entirety. Job experienced loss of monumental proportions. It was so bad that Job wanted to die. But he never gave up on seeing God. He knew he would be with God when he died.

It doesn't matter if you or I are struggling with severe financial problems, job loss, profound grief and heartache, major health problems, or relationship problems. It doesn't matter what it is; God will see us through it if we trust in Him like Job did. Job went through all of these things at one time, one right after the other. God brought him through every bit of it.

Reading the book of Job gave peace to my heart, strengthened my faith, and helped me feel close to God in my grief. I knew He was with me, with all of us, and would not leave us but would somehow see us through it. I held on as Job did and would not let go.

Part IV

FROM HEAVEN TO EARTH

IT'S LIKE THE WIND

I was still reeling. So much had happened in such a short amount of time, and so many of our lives were changed for the remainder of our time here on this earth ... *never* to be the same again.

Jeremy is dead, so is Amanda, and Joe is in the hospital in intensive care; Jeremy's death is being used as an example for the county teens, and just hours after the accident, his wrecked, demolished car is wanted for a display by many. Jeremy came to give me a goodbye hug after his death and before I even knew he was gone. Amanda's mother, Rosemary, has called and given the ultimate gifts of mercy and forgiveness.

We have switched gears from planning a party to planning a funeral. God Himself, through His great Holy Spirit, directed my open Bible to a very appropriate spot and then shed light on this spot with His flashlight of truth, and I knew without a doubt that it was the scripture that was to be read at Jeremy's funeral.

God held and rocked me in His big rocking chair, allowing me to feel His presence, His peace, and His love that is greater than any love on this earth because He is love. He guided me to His child Job, and He showed me how He was still in control no matter what was happening in Job's life.

And all of this happened in less than a forty-eight hour period. These are the beginnings of the Holy Spirit's comforting presence. After He sends more spiritual comforts to me in the next coming months, He guides me to another wonderful friend that I have. I don't know him personally, but

ROAD TRIP: JESUS, JEREMY AND ME

I have learned more about him through the guidance of the Holy Spirit. This man is alive today in heaven, and someday I will meet him too. His name is Nicodemus.

The Lord taught me about the powerful conversation that He had with Nicodemus and how it applied to me. It seems appropriate to include this now, instead of later. The things that were happening to me were spiritual, and since it is impossible for us to understand the spiritual world completely, and we wonder how it works with us, the Lord showed me that Nicodemus didn't understand it either even though he was Israel's teacher.

I have known the story of Nicodemus since I was a child, but I had not pondered it in my heart. I have learned that the Holy Spirit teaches me more and more as I ponder, meditate, and study His Word, and as I ask, seek, and knock, so I turned to John, chapter 3 to find out what the Lord wanted to show me.

John tells of an exciting time in history when a prominent religious teacher was moved to do something that went against his group's beliefs about the coming of the Messiah. Talk about a man having courage, he had it. Talk about listening to yourself instead of listening to others, he did it. Talk about going along with the crowd, he wouldn't. Talk about putting God first in his life, he proved it. This decision was based on his gut feelings, and his heart, and his mind. He acted on them. He told Jesus that he knew no one could do miraculous signs like He was doing if God were not with him. He was honest with Jesus about how he felt. This man's name was Nicodemus.

He came to see Jesus after dark one night. He had some questions for Jesus. Of course, he was doing this in secret and in the dark because he didn't want to get caught by the Jewish ruling council. This was the religious group that Nicodemus was a leader and member of.

Nicodemus had some detective work he wanted to do. The other members in the group did not like Jesus. They thought Jesus was nothing but trouble. That was just the way they saw it. They couldn't see that Jesus was the Messiah. They couldn't see that He was the one the Jews had been waiting for all those thousands of years, according to the scriptures. They couldn't accept it because they didn't want to recognize Jesus, no matter how many miracles He performed. They did not like Him! In fact, they hated Jesus. They were jealous of Him.

Nicodemus was different. He wanted to know more. He wanted to know the truth. I admire him so much for seeking the truth. He wanted to talk to Jesus about the miracles He was performing. He just knew that Jesus came from God because of these very miracles. He had no doubt about that, unlike the other members of his group.

When Jesus lived on this earth, He was a forgiving, humble, compassionate, loving man. However, He was no doormat to walk on. Oh no, He wasn't. He used a variety of approaches when dealing with people, depending on what each individual needed. His answers were custom-made for each person. Yes, custom-made. He knows us inside and out and knows exactly what we need. He did not hold back the truth. Ever! He has not changed! He treats us the same way. He is the same forever. He never tolerated sin. He was wise. He was genuine. He always stood on truth. He was and is truth. He was and is the Son of God, and He knew and knows precisely how to handle each and every situation with each and every person. When we study about Jesus, we learn that He knew exactly what to do.

Sometimes He was blunt and straightforward, and sometimes He wasn't.

Sometimes He spoke in parables, and other times He asked them questions.

Sometimes He told something to someone that nobody, nobody in the whole wide world, could possibly know—except him.

Sometimes He accused, and sometimes He didn't.

There were times He helped people think for themselves.

Sometimes He was gentle, and sometimes He was powerful.

Sometimes He gave them a miracle, and sometimes He told them what they needed to do to get a miracle.

He knew people's motives.

He knew people's hearts.

He knew people's struggles.

He knew everything about them, what they needed and how they needed it.

So, how did Jesus relate to Nicodemus?

Well, He didn't answer Nicodemus's interest in His miracles at first. No, He didn't. He had so much to teach Nicodemus about religion! Oh my, my! He knew Nicodemus was searching for answers. Nicodemus is a religious leader, but he didn't know about his own spirit. Jesus is about to blow him away with new information! Jesus wanted to talk to him about the kingdom of God and how Nicodemus could get there. This was the most important thing. This threw Nicodemus for a loop. Jesus started talking about being born again and being born of water and the Spirit. What?

"How can a man be born when he is old?" Nicodemus asked. "Surely he can't enter a second time into his mother's womb to be born" (John 3:4 NIV).

Jesus tells Nicodemus that it is not about fleshly birth. It is about the new birth of our spirits. He wanted Nicodemus to quit thinking about his physical body and think about his spirit. We know we are souls/spirits. We live inside these physical bodies. Our souls/spirits are who we are inside these bodies. It is who we really are. It is the part of us that will live forever in eternity. Our souls/spirits include our minds (not our physical brains), our hearts, which is our true emotional selves (not our physical hearts), our wills, our intentions, our attitudes, and our personalities. It is everything that we are without the physical body. We say we have a soul, but the truth is … we are souls. We say we have a soul so that we can distinguish the physical from the spiritual. The soul is not something that we can just be vaguely aware of. It's not something that just belongs to the future in thinking of it only as in death. It is life … here, right now, and later, and forever. It is who we are. When these houses of ours (physical bodies) breathe their last breath, we (our souls) leave. We must have somewhere to go! All of our loved ones who have passed on have done exactly that. They have moved out of their bodies and have continued living. The part of us that will sleep (death) is our physical bodies. When we die, if we want to live forever with God, Jesus says our souls/spirits must be "born again." He told Nicodemus that he must be born again of water and of the Spirit if he wanted to be a part of the kingdom of God.

John the Baptist was already baptizing people for the remission of their sins at that time in history. Nicodemus already knew about John's work. God had already instituted baptism by water. This was an outwardly, physical, voluntary action that could be seen with human eyes. This action showed repentance and obedience. God had sent John ahead of Jesus to prepare the way for the Messiah's coming. This was to get the people ready, to get them to think about their sins, because the Messiah was coming to die for their (our) sins. John preached about sin, and the people realized they were sinful in God's sight. He baptized them, showing their repentance and their wanting to be clean of sin. If we won't admit we are sinners, if we don't care that we are sinning, then Jesus's dying on the cross for our sins won't mean anything to us. Confession of our being sinful and repentance in our hearts, minds, and souls comes before baptism. Surrendering to God comes before baptism. Jesus said it was important to be baptized by water to be in the kingdom of God. Jesus was even baptized by John to live as an example for us to follow. God was pleased about Jesus wanting to be baptized. God took baptism a step further when His only begotten Son was baptized by water. Something utterly fantastic happened. This something had never ever happened to anyone before when John had baptized other people. No, it hadn't.

This fantastic something that happened was ... that ... the Holy Spirit came to Jesus!

"As soon as Jesus was baptized, he went up out of the water. At that moment heaven was opened, and he saw the Spirit of God descending like a dove and lighting on him. And a voice from heaven said, 'This is my Son, whom I love; with Him I am well pleased'" (Matthew 3:16–17 NIV).

When I studied that verse, something jumped out at me. Baptism was such a monumental event in Jesus's life that ... oh my, my, my ... wow, oh wow ... heaven ... opened! I just had to stop and ponder on that one! I wonder what it was like when heaven opened. It had to be a blessed, awe-inspiring, mighty moment of time in the history of humankind.

God was watching His only begotten Son as He was baptized. I remember how I felt when my children were baptized. It was such a blessed, fulfilling, wondrous, proud moment for me when they believed in Jesus and wanted to be baptized. I watched as they came up out of the water, and grateful, happy tears were in my eyes. I was very pleased and touched to the depths of my soul.

Well, God was very pleased with His Son too when He was baptized. There was action going on in heaven when this happened. When Jesus came up out of the water, God opened heaven. Here came the Holy Spirit like a dove. He came right down to light on Jesus. God spoke. God told

His Son and everybody else there how pleased He was. This was a unity and a display of the Holy Trinity at work, who is God the Father, Jesus the Son, and the Holy Spirit ... the great Three in One. Jesus the Son was baptized, God the Father spoke, and the Holy Spirit came down to rest on Jesus! Oh, how beautiful! Hallelujah!

It means so much to God that if we believe in His Son, Jesus, He will give us His Holy Spirit to live inside us when we show it by repentance of our sins and we are obedient to Him in baptism. It shows we want to change inside (we want to be born again). The Holy Spirit helps us in that change (new birth).

Well, back to Nicodemus. Jesus was teaching Nicodemus about the Holy Spirit and His work in us. Well, at first, Nicodemus's mind couldn't comprehend such a thing, but Jesus explained to him that this has nothing to do with the physical; it has everything to do with the spiritual. He chided Nicodemus for not understanding. After all, Nicodemus was one of Israel's religious leaders! He had studied the scripture, yet he didn't really understand what religion was all about! Jesus was teaching him what it was about. Jesus was the way to gain this new birth.

Once we receive Jesus into our hearts, and after we are baptized, we receive the gift of the Holy Spirit (Acts 2:38). We are born again of water and the Spirit. Baptism shows that we are willing to be made new. We are new born babes in Jesus Christ. We have a lot to learn and a lot to do just like new babies do. We accomplish these things as we grow in Christ. The Holy Spirit starts helping us to live the Christian life. He works from inside of us. We have to have His help with this because in our human nature alone, we cannot do it. So how does the Holy Spirit work inside of us with our spirits?

Jesus told Nicodemus that it was ... like the wind.

The Holy Spirit is invisible. Well, how is He like the wind? The wind is invisible. Even though the wind is invisible, it does lots of things that we physically see. We feel the wind, we hear the wind, and we can see the results of the wind, but we don't actually see the wind itself with our physical eyes. We have fancy technology that shows us some things about the wind, and we might know it is coming, but there are still times it sneaks up on us, and sometimes it changes its course and goes a different way. We say the wind sings, howls, moans, groans, and whistles. We say it blows, tosses, whips, rages, and devastates. We feel the gentle breezes, and we see the devastation after a tornado. I cannot imagine life without wind, can you? Our final analysis is the fact that we definitely know the wind does exist even though we cannot actually see the wind itself.

It is the same with the work of the Holy Spirit. Our spirits feel Him inside. Our spirits hear His gentle voice inside. We see the results of His working as a person changes. We become new creatures in Christ, because now He lives in us and helps us to become brand-new inside. We are new spiritual babies. As babes in Christ, our spirits start growing and learning God's way of living through the study of His Word with the Holy Spirit leading, teaching, and guiding through the newness. The Holy Spirit works with the Holy Word of God. Studying the Bible is essential in this transformation process. A person starts letting the Word of God and the Holy Spirit lead his or her life. Transformation begins in the life of the soul and expresses itself through the physical. It is a spiritual birth. The person starts to produce good fruit in his or her life. The good fruit of the Holy Spirit is love, joy, peace, patience, kindness, goodness, faithfulness, gentleness, and self-control (Galatians 5:22).

When we see these good things in a person's life, we know it is the Holy Spirit at work. The person now has hope and faith of living with God forever and is a part of the kingdom of God. We are royalty now. That sure puts earthly things in perspective!

Jesus gave the profound truth to Nicodemus in this nutshell of a sermon. He gave him all the information Nicodemus needed to know to live forever with God. He gave the truth that explained the past, present, and the future of all humankind. The present was right there as they spoke together, because Jesus the Messiah had come to earth. The past was in the prophecies that Nicodemus was supposed to have known. They predicted the Messiah's coming down to earth to save humankind. The future was that Jesus was going to die on the cross for our sins and then be raised up in three days to live forever and reign forever. Jesus wanted Nicodemus to *think* and put the puzzle together in a complete picture of the past, present, and future!

When Jesus and Nicodemus started talking, Jesus didn't talk about how He performed His miracles. He started talking about the kingdom of God. Jesus went right to the point, telling him what was really important

ROAD TRIP: JESUS, JEREMY AND ME

about Himself and His work. His mission was not about miracles. His mission was to bring people into His kingdom. These miracles were instruments in His real work, which was bringing people to Him, to His kingdom, which is the kingdom of heaven, which is our true home.

Nicodemus was witness to lots of these miracles! He was right there! Yet he found all of this very difficult to understand. He was using only his brain to try to figure it out, which is a useless attempt. When we see the devastation from the wind of a tornado, we are in awe of its power. Our brains cannot comprehend such power. When the people saw Jesus heal a paralyzed person, they were in awe. Their brains did not have the capacity to figure it out. That is because it is not a matter of our physical understanding; it is a matter of *believing* in the power of the unseen Holy Spirit at work. The people didn't understand, yet they were drawn to Jesus because they knew these things were really happening. They saw it with their own eyes. He was drawing them to Him so they could get to know Him. He was revealing to them that He was the Messiah.

Nicodemus was talking to the Son of God. He was there. Jesus was sent by God, given by God, and fathered by God. He was the miracle. He was God in the flesh, coming down from heaven, born of a virgin. He was a living, breathing, walking, talking miracle given to us in love. He was the one, the one they had been waiting for. In fact, they had waited for thousands of years for this very person, and Nicodemus was standing right beside the one they had been waiting for! He was sitting with Him while He explained where He came from, who He was, how the Holy Spirit works, what to do to get Him. Nicodemus was talking to God in the flesh.

This conversation between these two men had and still has for us today a monumental impact that cannot be ignored. It was built on this one foundation that Jesus is getting ready to tell Nicodemus. It is one of the most beloved verses of all time.

"For God so loved the world that He gave His one and only Son, that whoever believes in him shall not perish but have eternal life" (John 3:16 NIV).

I am looking forward to seeing Nicodemus when I get to heaven. I admire him so much for having the courage to go talk to Jesus in the best way he could, which was in the very dark of night. I admire him for letting go of his own ego so he could listen and learn. I admire him for asking, seeking, and knocking to get answers. He didn't just go along with the crowd and what they thought. I admire that too. That isn't easy. I admire him for being a religious leader who wanted to put God first. Nicodemus was a fine man, and Jesus knew it. I can just imagine Jesus and Nicodemus being together having this great and mighty talk that has never grown old in over two thousand years, and not only that, it has reached out to touch the entire world. I can just imagine the earnestness on Nicodemus's face as he takes this all in, sorts through it, ponders it, and thinks deeply about it. I can just see the light come into his eyes when the recognition of the truth … the recognition of who Jesus is … sinks into his mind, heart, and soul. When he realized it was the Messiah teaching him about the scriptures, it was a moment in time never to forget! It was a conversation for the world, never to be forgotten, recorded in the Holy Bible. It was a pulling together of the Old Testament and the New Testament to make the Holy Bible whole and complete. The Holy Bible, God's baby book from beginning to end, is about His Son. It is about His Son who came to earth to save us from the evil one. It is His baby book not only for His only begotten Son but also for all of us who are His children. It is our baby book too!

It is so thrilling to think that one day I will see the very people who are in the Bible. They are family! I will see Nicodemus one day face-to-face, get to know him and talk about that night so long ago when he got to be a part of history that changed the entire world. I am so looking forward to meeting my spiritual brother Nicodemus.

Why did God want me to study, ponder, and meditate on the conversation between Jesus and Nicodemus? Because He wanted me to know that the spiritual experiences that He was sending to me were like the wind! I didn't physically see any of it, but I knew, felt, and heard them with my spiritual eyes, my spiritual ears, and my spiritual heart and mind. This is who I really am. I am soul/spirit. The Holy Spirit was at work in my soul. The Holy Spirit was sending miracles to me. Oh, how thankful I was. I knew the miracles I was receiving were real and that heaven had surrounded me. I knew they were the works of the great Holy Spirit, the Comforter who lives inside of me. They happened just like Jesus explained it to Nicodemus. This is how the Holy Spirit works. He said, "It's like the wind." Every miracle that the Lord gave me was like the wind blowing

ROAD TRIP: JESUS, JEREMY AND ME

through me, leaving me unexpected gifts. Nothing could be seen with the physical eyes, but they were real all the same. Each of them brought me knowledge, love, comfort, and joy. Praise the Living God. I was filled with awe.

I am in awe of the Holy Spirit's work. He is invisible, yet He leaves His mark in the world through His work. Praise God!

The full account of the conversation between Jesus and Nicodemus is found in John 3:1–18.

AMAZING GRACE

I knew God was in control, but oh, how my heart ached.
I went to my heavenly Father in prayer. "How do I go to the funeral home and be with my child's body?" I cried.

I didn't think I could do it. The thought of it was agony. The pain was excruciating.

God answered my prayer.

The thought came to me that Jesus knew all about the agony of physical death. I knew this thought was from the Holy Spirit. I was not alone in my pain. This was the Holy Spirit helping me remember that Jesus was inside of me and would be going with me, and He would grieve with me. Jesus knows how hard death separation is for us and the ones we love. I was reminded how He grieved for Lazarus when he died. It was when Jesus went to Lazarus's tomb that he broke down.

He wept for Lazarus (John 11:34–36 NIV).

I had learned from the death of my child what it means to weep. Weeping is much more than crying. Weeping comes from deep, deep within. Jesus wept long enough and hard enough that the people there saw how much He loved Lazarus. They were touched by it. Jesus's heart also went out to Mary, Martha, and the others as He saw them weeping in grief. He hurt for them just like He hurts for us when we hurt. This has not changed.

The Holy Spirit kept showing me how Jesus was very familiar with grief. Jesus experienced unimaginable pain, knowing He was going to leave his beloved disciples. This was His human emotions. He hurt just like we do. The Holy Spirit drew me to read and study John, chapter 14. Jesus did a wonderful thing for His disciples. He started preparing them and comforting them about His own death that was to come. He knew they didn't understand what was going to happen to Him. It was too much to tell them all at once. He knew it would overwhelm them. He spoke in ways that were baffling at times. However, He knew they would remember His words after He was gone. The Holy Spirit would see to that. He would help them understand when the time came. Jesus loved His disciples with all his mind, heart, and soul. He knew how much they could bear at one time. He told them He was going away, but He would not leave them as orphans. Well, what did that mean?

For three years they had been His followers and His friends. They had given up everything to follow Him. He was their life! He had been their leader, guide, teacher, comforter, friend, and more. They had given up everything for Him, and He was everything to them! They had been with and lived with the Messiah, the Lord of Lords, the King of Kings, and the Prince of Peace. They had been with God in the flesh on earth. It doesn't get any better than that down here! He knew they were going to be devastated by His death, but He wanted them to know he would not leave them as orphans. He would be in them, they would be in Him, and He would send the Holy Spirit to them (John 14:18–20 NIV).

Jesus started talking more about His coming death. This is found in John 16. The disciples had just acknowledged that Jesus came from God. He asked them if this was their final acknowledgment. Did this mean that they would be brave enough to stick with Him to the very end? They thought they could, and they thought they would. Each of them thought they would, especially Peter. Of course, they did not know what this was going to mean for them personally when it all came down to the life and death of their own selves. They had no idea how this was going to play out. Again, it is easy to talk the talk but hard when walking the walk. It is an entirely different story when we are put to the actual test. I know I have eaten my words plenty of times.

Jesus knew how it was going to end. He knew how they were going to scatter, each of them running for their own lives to their own homes as fast as they could get there, scared to death. They weren't even going to stick together. They were going to leave Him totally alone to fight His own battle. He knew this ahead of time, yet He had understanding and compassion for them. He told them right up front they would desert Him, and then He told them not to worry about it. What?

He told His disciples not to worry about Him and told them *why* they didn't have to worry about Him. He said they didn't have to worry about Him because He would not be alone. He wanted them to know that His Father would be with Him. His very own Father would not desert Him.

Jesus knew His disciples' grief was going to be bad. He knew how it was going to be, and He did not want to add guilt to their souls about deserting Him. He did not want them to live in torment because they had left Him all alone. He wanted them to have peace, so He assured them that He would not be alone, that God His Father would be with Him. He knew that if they stayed in torment over this, they would not be able to do the work that He had for them to do after He was gone. His assurance gave them strength to battle the grief of losing Him physically from this world. This is the amazing grace of our Lord Jesus Christ. This is the amazing grace from God our Father. God gave forgiveness to these disciples for deserting His Son in the worst time of His life. And before it even happened! He knew it was going to happen, and God and Jesus both gave forgiveness and wonderful assurance to these disciples.

God wanted me to know that I would not be going to the funeral home without Him. He would be with me, Jesus would be with me, and the Holy Spirit would be with me. The Holy Trinity knows all about grief and agony. God gave me wonderful, blessed assurances to battle the grief of losing Jeremy from this world. He had already allowed Jeremy to hug me good-bye after his physical death. The spiritual goodbye hug was the first blessed assurance. The second one happened at the funeral home.

I knew there was no way out of this situation. I had to face going to the funeral home. We were told that Jeremy might not look like himself because he had such extensive injuries. I did not know how I was going to look at him, yet I knew I wanted to. I didn't know how I was going to stand it, so I had worked at mentally preparing myself for the visitation. What I thought would happen did not happen. What I prepared for did not happen.

You see, all I wanted to do was hold him. I was certain that if people did not hold me back, I would try to get Jeremy out of that casket and hold him in my arms.

I have to say, I would have never … I would have never … ever … imagined … what did actually happen. I was totally unprepared for it, but I tell you the truth: it happened so naturally that I never even thought to question anything about it. Not one thing!

As I stood in front of the casket for the first time and looked down at him, the only thing that mattered was what happened next.

He was not there in the casket. I knew his body would be there, but his soul would be gone, so this was no surprise. However, he *was* there! His soul/spirit was above me! Yes, he was!

"Oh, my faithful, wonderful, awesome God, what a blessed miracle you gave me!"

I felt Jeremy's spirit above me, and he was very close to the top of my head. He was hovering over me, and he spoke to me! He said four short sentences.

"I'm up here.

"I'm not down there in that body.

"I'm up here watching over you.

"I'm okay."

It was real. He spoke with authority, and it was powerful!

Well, my reaction was as simple and trusting as a child's is! I nodded my head and responded by saying, "Okay."

I answered him out loud!

I nodded my head to him!

I told my sister, Karen, who was standing beside me, that I was ready to sit down. I sat down calmly thinking about how the Lord had softened the blow. I felt as if I was in another world. I basked in His love, His peace, feeling the security of being His child.

It was a moment of amazing grace. I knew that Jeremy's spirit was with all of us, and God was allowing him to help us each step of the way. God had not left me alone. He was present with me, His child. He allowed the spiritual world to open up to the physical world. The Comforter, the Great Holy Spirit, was at work in this.

I didn't tell anybody what had happened at that moment. I was in my own little world basking in the knowledge of what Jeremy had told me and basking in the feeling of his presence with me and basking in the love and peace that my Father in heaven had sent to me. It was inside me, outside me, and all around me.

I don't claim to understand it, but I accepted it as another of God's great gifts. God doesn't owe me an explanation. Just as He told Job, He answers to nobody. He is God. Praise His holy name!

It was what Jesus had told Nicodemus. It was real, like the wind. I felt it, I heard it, and I knew it in my mind, I knew it in my heart, and I knew it in my soul. I knew I had received a blessed assurance from the Father in heaven.

This did not stop the pain. Oh no, it did not. But I could handle the pain in my heart with peace in my soul. There were times of anguished weeping coming from that place that resides so deep inside me. You know that place I told you about, from that new place that I never knew about before this happened. I had not known of its existence. I had entered this sacred place and would stay there for a long time. My sobs came from the depths of my soul, where there did not seem to be a beginning or an end … because there is none. I let it out. I couldn't have kept this pain inside of me if I had tried to. It poured from me when I least expected it. It was like a spewing volcano exploding from within me. It came like waves crashing upon the beach during a hurricane, wave after wave of grief. Grief is so consuming. It is such hard work. Separation from Jeremy was like being ripped apart inside with parts of me leaving and flying away from me, and there was no way to stop them from leaving.

Between the periods of weeping, God gave me rest to get ready for the next wave of grief. It was in the resting that I had peace, knowing that Jeremy was not all alone in death. It was in the resting that I knew beyond a shadow of a doubt that He was and is okay. It was in the resting that I knew that God had allowed Jeremy to stay beside us to comfort us. These were miracles, true workings of the Holy Spirit. I am deeply touched even now, twenty years later. I praise God for His amazing grace. He did not leave me as an orphan at the funeral home. He did not leave me in my battle of grief. He came to me.

> "I will not leave you as orphans;
> I will come to you."
> —John 14:18 (NIV)

SWEET AMANDA

We left the funeral home where Jeremy lay and went to another funeral home in another town to be with Amanda's parents. We had never met Rosemary and Steve. I had only talked on the phone to Rosemary.

Again, there were no words we could say that were adequate. We could only offer our presence and extend our heavy-hearted sorrow to them for what had happened. We embraced, and we felt their genuineness and the fact that they grieved for our loss as well as their own. We were two sets of parents, each in deep sorrow ourselves and in deep sorrow for each other. We knew each other's pain, and it was so heavy.

It was at the Last Supper that Jesus gave His disciples a new commandment. He said for them to love each other as much as He loved them. He went on to say that this would prove to the world that they were His disciples (John 13–34).

I am witness to the fact that I felt this kind of love from these people that I didn't even know. It was the proof that Jesus was teaching about.

Love is truly proof of discipleship. We felt it not only from Amanda's parents and her brothers and sisters but also from her extended family on both sides. There was a sweet, sweet spirit in that place. That sweet spirit was the Holy Spirit of God.

We talked about our children. We had lots of unanswered questions. None of us knew why Jeremy and Amanda were together, and none of us knew much about the events of that fateful night. We had no answers. I have to say at that time and place, the most important thing at the moment was the preciousness of our sweet children. That was all that mattered. It was almost as if we could hold this preciousness in our hands. The air was heavy with it.

We had never met Amanda, and they had never met Jeremy, so we shared memories, sorrow, and love. We learned what a beautiful girl Amanda was. Her spirit, her mind, and her heart were as beautiful as her physical beauty. I stared at her picture and saw she had a marvelous smile that absolutely lit up her face. We found out that Amanda was a poet. She wrote poetry that was rich in every word, and it was poetry that was full of wisdom and beauty that went well beyond her years.

In continuing months, I read her poetry often, and I wept, and I wept, and I wept. I read her poetry, and I learned from her. I knew that her poetry and words would live on and enrich many lives. I read her poetry and felt that I knew her heart. Amanda's life was proof of her discipleship; she portrayed to the world that truth was her guide and love was her greatest aim. I will meet her when it is my turn to go to heaven, and I will look forward to this with great anticipation. She is a part of my life now and will be forever. She is sewn into my heart. You see, my heart cried for Amanda, for Amanda's parents, for her brothers and sisters and for her extended family. I knew if Jeremy had been there, his heart would have been crushed and broken in pieces. I knew his heart was broken anyway in death, when he realized what had happened. We each have to give an account for our deeds and face God in heaven. This was a part of Jeremy's life here on earth, and he had taken this to heaven with him. It was the last earthly thing he did and was a part of him, and he could not erase it. Even though it is a part of him and always will be, Jesus covered it with His blood at the cross. Jeremy did not intentionally mean to hurt anybody. He had a tender heart and would have been mortified at the thought. Jesus knew (knows) his heart. Jesus met Amanda and Jeremy, taking care of them immediately. They were never alone in death. Jesus took care of everything from that moment on. There are no tears in heaven, no sorrow in heaven. God knows our hearts and knows who belongs to Him and why things happen the way they do. God was right there with His two children, Jeremy and Amanda, to meet them, to help them, and to comfort them.

He knew everything about the whole situation. He knew it was going to happen before it even happened. He never left them as orphans. The Holy Spirit was there and went to work immediately to bring heaven and earth together in the sorrowful moments that were to come.

Amanda knows how much I grieved for her and her family. I felt her love at that funeral home, and I still to this day feel her love. Her love is proof of her discipleship to the Lord. She fulfilled His command to "love one another." I love her too.

> "A new command I give you:
> Love one another.
> As I have loved you,
> so you must love one another.
> By this all men
> will know that you are my disciples,
> if you love one another."
> —John 13:34–35 (NIV)

OUR SWEET JEREMY

We returned to Jeremy and somehow made it through the next two days of visitation. We had lots of help in everything we did. Our families and friends stood by us faithfully. Jo Carol, one of our nieces, spent nights with us to help us survive them. Our nieces and nephews were very close to our hearts and still are. We needed them desperately to be with us at this time, and they were right there with us. Debbie, Sherry, Jo Carol, Wendy, Tony, Terry, Tracy, Chad, Christy, Lisa, Susie, Troy, Davy, and Amy were all so precious to us and were so much a part of our lives that their presence with us meant more than they will ever know. It still is that way and will always be. We have had some changes since Jeremy's death. We have another nephew who was born after Jeremy died; his name is Coby. He is a brother to Troy, Davy, and Amy, and he is very precious to us. The other change is that Jeremy's cousin Debbie died on New Year's Day of 2015. She took a nap and died in her sleep. It was a shock to all of us. We miss her very much. Jeremy and Debbie are together in heaven waiting for all of us to join them someday.

Funerals are a part of life. They are precious to us even though they are heartbreaking. I wrote a short note to Jeremy to be read at his funeral.

Dear Jeremy,

You always said you had to go. You had to see people

and talk to people. You said you wanted to be everywhere and with everybody. You loved all the towns in our county, and I would say there were probably many more places that you loved that we didn't know about. You did not play favorites; it seemed you loved people with no conditions or judgments attached. I know that Jesus would call this the unconditional love that He wants us to have for each other. You told me many times that you just had to go.

This is not the way we wanted your life to end, or the way you wanted it to end, but this is the way it is. Now, you can soar everywhere and be with everybody, because now you are a *free* bird.

Love,
Mom

I wrote this because this was Jeremy's life. He was constantly on the go and with people. Even though he was an introvert and very shy, he had this intense urging that sent him out to people.

At the age of thirteen, he started working on a dairy farm that belonged to the parents of his good friend Kevin. He became a part of that family. Kevin's mother, Judy, made sure she cooked food that Jeremy liked and treated him as one of her own. She made sure she had ketchup too! Everybody knew about Jeremy's love for ketchup. That family loved Jeremy, and he loved them. Jeremy and Kevin had lots of good times together. Jeremy loved Kevin's dad, Bobby, and his older brother, Brian, too. Jeremy was very happy working on their farm. This was in a community about seven miles from where we lived. I would take him there every afternoon after school, and Billy would go get him when his work was done. He worked there after school, on Saturdays, and in the summers for three years.

Our conversations during that short commute usually involved talking about land. Jeremy talked of saving money to buy a little piece of land to call his own, maybe an acre. He was young, and he thought that would be enough land for him at that time of his life. When he became of age, he could do what he wanted to with it, build a home there or use it for a camper getaway place. He had one problem with it. He could not make up his mind where he wanted it to be. He loved every community and town of our county. He would always say, "I want to be everywhere and with everybody."

It was only fitting that we played the song "Free Bird" by Lynyrd Skynyrd at his funeral. My brother, Ricky, suggested it and got it for us. It was one of Jeremy's favorite songs.

Our nephew Troy wanted to play a special song on the piano for Jeremy, and it was the most heavenly music that came forth from him. It was played from a heart full of love for his cousin. It was a beautiful funeral, if there is such a thing. Scott, our minister, gave a wonderful sermon fueled by passion and full of love, compassion, and concern for other teens. He was cut to the core over this, and his words conveyed his pain and suffering also. There was definitely a sweet, sweet spirit in the church. It was the sweet spirit of the Holy Spirit. Others told us they sensed Jeremy hovering over us during the entire service. We ended it with the song "Go Rest High on That Mountain" by Vince Gill. Jeremy's physical work on earth was finished. It was over. We laid his body to rest beside his Pappaw Ockerman.

The only piece of land Jeremy ever had was the ground where we buried him.

THE LETTER AND JEREMY'S POEM

It was the day after the funeral when JoAnn called. She had a special relationship with Jeremy. She had been the one to cut his hair for the past eight years, and believe me, getting his hair cut was a big deal to him. He was very particular about the way he wanted it cut and wouldn't leave until he was satisfied. JoAnn had told me many times that Jeremy intimidated her, but she always managed to please him. I don't remember Jeremy ever complaining about any haircut that he received from JoAnn. He made sure he was satisfied before he left the shop. JoAnn was very patient at working with him, which helped to create the very good relationship they had.

There were several people at our house that day. When the phone rang, it was my sister, Karen, who answered it. JoAnn told Karen that she had something special for us. She wanted us to have it right away. We lived in town, and JoAnn's shop was maybe a mile away, so Karen went to get the something that JoAnn felt was urgently special.

JoAnn had written us a letter explaining it. In fact, she had two letters that she wanted us to have. Karen brought the letters to our house and told me that JoAnn wanted me to read them as soon as possible. I simply could not focus enough to read them at that time, so I asked Karen to put them in a safe place. I thought I would read them later. A storm was brewing outside. Since it was a bad one, many of us went to our basement to wait it out. Some of the men were upstairs watching the storm, when one of them came and told us it had taken down the big tree in our front yard. The Lord got my attention with that tree falling in our front yard! It was then that I remembered the letters and was concerned for their safety. I asked Karen where the letters were, and she said she would run upstairs and get them. She brought them to me, and I started reading.

JoAnn had written a letter to us explaining that since Jeremy's death, she had been trying to write something comforting to send to us, but she couldn't come up with anything on her own. She had something though, and the something special she had for us was a poem. When I finished reading this letter from JoAnn, I had lots of questions in my mind. I was definitely anxious to read the poem she had written. I really hadn't known that JoAnn wrote poetry, so that was a surprise in itself. It seemed very important to her for us to have this poem. I thought it was odd that she said she didn't know how we would react to the poem. I couldn't imagine why she said that. I had to read on to see what this poem was about! I forgot all about the storm. I forgot about all the people at the house. I was totally into what JoAnn was saying. I had to read that poem. I was standing in our basement, and I remained standing as I read the poem. I finished reading it, and I was in awe of God's wonderful gift that He had sent. I just stood there in absolute amazement at what I was holding in my hands. I was holding a message from our son. It had come through JoAnn … like the wind! The Holy Spirit was truly at work in this poem and in JoAnn.

> There are different kinds of gifts,
> but the same Spirit.
> There are different kinds of service,
> but the same Lord.
> There are different kinds of working,
> but the same God works all of them in all men.
> —1 Corinthians 12:4–6 (NIV)

BLESSED ASSURANCE

There was only one word that I would use to describe how I felt after reading the poem from Jeremy. That one word was speechless. My mouth just automatically and completely fell open.

This poem was from Jeremy!

I had no doubt!

I showed it to Billy. After he read it, his mouth fell open just like mine had, and he was speechless just as I had been.

I got the very same reaction from Julie.

I got the same reaction from his cousin Lisa.

I got the same reaction from everybody else who read the poem.

The first thing they all did was look at me. Then their mouths fell open in amazement, and then they were speechless.

There was no doubt in anybody's mind that we had been given another blessed assurance from God the Father. It came from His precious Holy Spirit, the Comforter.

"Oh, my Father in heaven!" I cried. "Thank you, thank you, thank you!"

I could hardly wait to see JoAnn, so I went to see her the very next day. She was excited to see me and had so much she wanted to tell me! She said she had prayed to God to help her write something to us that would be of comfort. She said she couldn't come up with anything. She was working in her shop and had one customer under the hair dryer when all of a sudden she knew that Jeremy was with her. She felt his presence, and he told her what to write!

She said she wrote and wrote, only stopping one time. She stopped because he had stopped her. She had used the wrong word, and he wasn't satisfied with it! She changed the word and then went on with it. When she was finished, she was amazed at what she had written. She said she had held it as if it were a piece of gold. JoAnn said she had written poems for many years, but this one was nothing at all like her writings. She took it home with her because she wanted to ask her husband what he thought about it. She read it to him. She asked him if he thought she had written it. He said he didn't think she wrote it because it was not like the other things she had written. She told him she was the one who wrote it, and she told him how it happened. He was amazed!

Then she said after she had written it, Jeremy was restless and wanted her to get it to us as soon as possible. She called our house, and Karen answered the phone and then went and picked it up for us.

She wanted to know about the word she had used that he didn't like because she didn't understand why he didn't like it. She told me what the word was, and I knew what he meant. I am his mother and I understood the reason he wanted it changed. JoAnn said there were things in it that she did not even know about. We knew everything that was said in the poem was from Jeremy. There was no doubt then. There is still no doubt all these years later.

This was a great gift from God the holy Father, who can do anything and everything. There are no limits to His great power! Praise His holy name!

Jeremy assured us in the poem that he was okay and that he was with Jesus.

The poem is beautiful. It is spoken from Jeremy's heart, mind and soul and is a testimony of his love for his family, his friends, and his Lord. Everyone who has read the poem has been in awe. One of our friends, Marilyn, embroidered it and had it framed for us.

JoAnn expressed to me that she thought Jeremy was a gardener while he was on this earth. He sowed seeds everywhere he went and with everybody he met. The seeds took root in people's lives at the impact of his death. The seeds he sowed were seeds of love toward everyone. Isn't this one of the most loving compliments that could ever be bestowed upon another? Thank you, JoAnn! This is proof of Jeremy's discipleship. The poem is also proof of his discipleship.

I am thankful for JoAnn's prayer to God asking him to help her write something of comfort to us. I thank her for her openness to receiving the gift of the poem from Jeremy when God answered her prayer. I thank her for the courage it took for her to follow through with this. I thank her for her believing spirit, who was willing to be a vessel of God's unconditional love. I thank her for her love for God, her love for us, and her love for Jeremy. The things that were in the poem were Bible based. We can always know for sure that gifts are from God when they are in agreement with the Word of God.

I thank God for this beautiful gift He gave us before the lights went out, and we were drowning in sorrow.

Part V

DROWNING IN SORROW

GRADUATION

How do you go to a high school graduation service when your child is not here to graduate? What's the point of going anyway?

Well, there did seem to be a point. We wanted to go. It still was his graduation day. It seemed it helped with closure to twelve years of Jeremy's education. How we did that, I really don't know. I look back at it, and all I can say is that God was with us. There is no other explanation for it.

Of course, his cousins Lisa and Davy were graduating also. We knew this was really painful for them. This was supposed to be a joyous celebration for all, but it was mixed with grief for them and for all our families.

They had asked the principal and been given permission to accept Jeremy's diploma on his behalf. They were proud to accept it, and we were proud of them for wanting to do this for him. We watched as Jeremy's name was called and Davy and Lisa together proudly walked out to receive it. After the service, they brought it to us so we could take it home and put it with his other things.

We were all definitely still in a stage of shock that would come and go. Actually, that night, I know shock was our friend. It surrounded both sides of our families as we sat together through the service. I felt numb all over. I did not shed a tear. In fact, I don't remember seeing any tears on the faces of our families. Shock and numbness were our protectors that night to get us through it.

After it was over, there were so many loving people who came to us to share our experience. They had tears and plenty of them. They had been praying for us to get through this, and it worked. God was with us. That is how we got through it.

I remember a lady that I didn't know, but she knew Jeremy. He was friends with her son and had been to her house. She came up to me and kissed my face with tears streaming down hers. She put kisses all over my face. She hugged me and didn't want to let go. She was so compassionate in her sorrow that I will never ever forget her. I don't know her, but I love her.

Graduation was over. Jeremy's life was over. It was done. It was time to go home.

THE LIGHTS GO OUT

We went home without Jeremy.
He was gone.

The first week without him, it seemed as if I was suspended between heaven and earth. Heaven seemed close and all around me. It seemed as if loved ones who had already passed were very close by me. I felt them. It was a place I had never been before, and it was enclosed with a specialness that was wonderful. One other thing that really seemed changed was nature. I had never seen nature like this before in my entire life. It was as if I could see nature through more spiritual eyes than my physical eyes; for instance, the grass was a sparkling, rich green that I had never seen before. Colors were totally vivid, and the air seemed fresher than usual. I wasn't the only one who saw a difference. Billy saw and felt it, too. This seemed to be especially true in our backyard. It was brighter and more alive than we had ever experienced it. We marveled at it and questioned such exquisite beauty. It is very hard to describe it. In fact, I think words are useless here because I don't know any words that are adequate. It was almost as if we could see and feel the throb of life that seemed to be in every living thing. I have never to this day experienced anything like that before or since. It was a short time of being in a safe, serene, beautiful place. That was another gift that had been sent to us by God Almighty. This lasted for about a week after the funeral. It is from this experience that now I realize the prince of darkness hides this beauty from our physical eyes. Oh, yes, he does. This spiritual beauty is here because I have seen it, if only for a brief time. God is in every living thing. It is a wonder to behold! However, Satan works constantly to keep us in darkness, to shut out the light at all times. He likes to keep us in the dark, and that is exactly what happened next.

Everything went dark. Who pulled the plug, the gigantic plug that keeps the world going? Who turned out the lights? It was so very, very, very dark. I'm telling you, it was the darkest of dark. This darkness was in our souls. It was awful. It was so dark in our souls that we had to have a nightlight on so we could sleep at night. We just couldn't bear that horrible darkness. The darkness was so thick it seemed we couldn't breathe. The darkness was suffocating; it was choking; it was consuming, and it was terrifying. There was death in that darkness, whose name is Satan.

The nights were horrible, and the days were torture. During the day, I felt as if the world had stopped completely. It was as if it had come to a sudden halt, frozen in time. It either stopped, or I got off. I wasn't sure which had happened. I didn't feel a part of the world anymore. I felt that I was flung out of it and far away from it. I had been disconnected from the world. Nothing looked real, and nothing seemed real. Sometimes people looked like robots moving around everywhere, and I was frozen in place. At other times, it seemed as if all people were frozen, and I was the only one moving. No matter which way life seemed to be working, I did not feel a part of it.

I also felt confused. Who died? Did Jeremy die or did I die? The confusion was great. Reality would come and go. I was being attacked by grief, attacked in every way possible: physically, emotionally, mentally, and spiritually. This was war! Satan loves what death does to loved ones, and he goes to work with all his might using all his artillery. He had thrust his sword, and that was just the beginning of his cruel attack and his claim on us. It was only the beginning of the battle. He started throwing his fiery darts, and God sent His blessed assurances. There was intense spiritual warfare going on.

There were times I felt I was barely hanging on to my life by my fingertips. There were things I was dealing with that made me think I was going crazy. I couldn't even look in the mirror at my own reflection. It caused intense pain just to *look* at myself.

I cried, "Oh, Lord God Almighty, why can't I even look in the mirror?"

Road Trip: Jesus, Jeremy and Me

I couldn't spend very much time on my hair. Brush and go, and I don't have that kind of hair! I couldn't look long enough to put on makeup. And I was a Mary Kay lady! I loved my makeup, but it was too painful to look. Looking at my own face caused a gush of tears that didn't make any sense. Looking at my own face hurt my heart, and I would turn away from the mirror as fast as I could.

I kept crying out to God for help. I wouldn't give up.

"Oh, dear God," I cried. "I feel like I'm going crazy. Please help me, please, please, please help me." I was begging, pleading for help. I felt like melting into a puddle on the floor.

God did help me. I can't say it was immediate relief because it wasn't. It came as time went by. Little by little, He sent information to me in various ways about the grief experienced when losing a child. I found out that these feelings I was experiencing were normal. Just finding out that these feelings were normal was an absolute Godsend. It was normal to feel pain when I looked in the mirror! I was normal. That helped a lot to know that! There were reasons for this pain. It was so painful to look in the mirror because I did not recognize myself when I looked in the mirror! What? Well, why not?

Because I was not the same person that I was before!

My life had changed completely, and this had changed me completely! This helped me to know that I wasn't losing my mind. It was many months before I could actually look in the mirror long enough to apply makeup and work with my hair. It wasn't that I didn't care about my appearance; it was the fact that I couldn't even *look*. Healing had to do its job first.

Also, at this time, I had the strong desire to shave my head. Shave my head! Well, where did that come from? It was an intense desire that I didn't understand. Instead of having my head shaved, I asked JoAnn to cut it very short. This helped even though I don't like short hair on myself. Now, I know why people in the Old Testament time shaved their heads and put on sackcloth and ashes during grieving. If I had had some sackcloth and ashes, I would have used them. I understand now, because it all came from a desire that was deep, deep inside of me to throw away my old self, because I had changed. I couldn't be that old self again. I couldn't go back to the way I was. God sent information as needed. I don't know that I could have figured this out on my own. Knowing why I felt this way helped me significantly. Grieving was changing me. So I came to be at peace with my mirror and my short hair while I was healing.

Then the water came crashing over me. Oh, yes, I mean waves and waves of water. I was drowning in it. I could not hold my head above the water. I was sinking. This was not a nightmare. This was happening during the day when I was awake. I was absolutely suffocating in the drowning, and it felt as real as real can be.

Was I going crazy? I just knew I wouldn't live through this, because I was going to drown. Thankfully, God gave me information about that. This sensation of drowning was normal too! I was drowning in sorrow. I didn't know that. I didn't know I could feel that I was drowning from my sorrow and grief. Grief affects the lungs, and my lungs were struggling big-time. There have been people who have died from grief. Now I understand why.

King David faced these waters in his torment and grief. He asked God to reach down His hand from on high and deliver him. He said the waters were up to his neck. He asked to be rescued from the mighty waters (Psalm 69:1–2 and Psalm 144:7).

I felt as if I was going completely under because I didn't have the strength to stay above the water. It was then that I felt strong arms around me. I looked, and there was Jeremy holding me up on one side and Jesus holding me up on the other side until Satan let go and I could swim to the shore and get out of the terrifying water. They protected me and held my head above the swirling, dangerous water. The Holy Spirit showed me that spiritually, mentally, physically, and emotionally, I was held up by my Savior and my son during this terrifying trip into deep waters of sorrow. This could have killed me. I was in this darkness for a long time. It would come and go. I would have rest from it at times as I worked my way out of the swirling, turbulent waters of grief.

There was so much pain in this sorrow, and added to that were the relentless reporters from the newspaper. They wanted to see Jeremy's report from his autopsy so they could write another story. We were advised by many not to read his autopsy report because it would only add to our pain. It would be too cold, too detailed and would put us through more unnecessary pain. We still to this day do not know the extent of our son's injuries. We never looked at the wrecked car. It took a full year before we could even go to the spot where the wreck happened.

We were thankful to God. We did have lots of people who cared about us. They helped to protect us. Love came from those who helped to spare us from as much pain as possible on top of everything else we had endured. I look back now in utter amazement at all the support we had from our community, and my heart overflows with gratitude and thankfulness at the good in people, at the love in people.

It made me stop and think about my Savior. I knew God was talking to me again and wanted me to think about something. I knew that Jesus did not have this protection when He died. He was deserted. I couldn't imagine what He felt like when He was deserted. He was alone. Nobody understood what He was going through except His Father. His Father did not spare Himself the ugliness of pain and sorrow due to the cruelty and death to His only begotten Son. Father God saw all, felt all, and understood all.

He watched while His only begotten Son was beaten. He watched the trial as Jesus, who was His only Son and the Perfect One was accused of wrongdoing, and He knew His Son was innocent! He knew it, yet He stood back! He saw men put deep lashes on His Son's back, and His Son had done nothing wrong. He saw them spit in Jesus's face. He saw them jab thorns on His Son's brow. He saw them hammer those nails in His Son's hands and feet. He saw Him nailed to that cross. He knew the pain and agony His Son was in. He had the power to stop every bit of it, but He didn't.

Why didn't He stop it?

He didn't stop it because He loves us that much.

He loved His Son so much, but He loves us too. What love! He watched and did nothing while His Child was murdered for us ... to save us. But it was painful. When Jesus was dying on the cross, everything went dark. When I say everything, I mean the whole earth. The lights went out! The whole earth was covered in darkness for three whole hours. This happened from noon until 3:00 p.m. I cannot imagine what it was like for the people on earth when that darkness hit. This is recorded in three different places: Matthew 27:45, Mark 15:33, Luke 23:44.

The light from the sun was gone for three whole hours. Satan was in that darkness. He thought he had victory over the world now. He was satisfied. Humans had murdered the Son of God. Satan's victory was short-lived though. Actually, it wasn't any kind of victory at all because it was the plan. When Jesus's sacrificial work was finished, He came back to life. The world was dark for three hours when Jesus hung on the cross, and Jesus came back to life again on day three after His death.

We can be forgiven for all of our horrible sins. Jesus covered that at the cross. He took them away. God took our sins upon Himself so we could be made whiter than snow in his sight. This does not keep us from the fiery darts that Satan throws at us while we are here on earth. Oh no! No, it does not. It does not keep us from temptation. It does not! It does not take away pain and sorrow during grief. No, it does not! What does it do? It gives us comfort and strength in our suffering. It gives peace that is beyond our understanding.

God was victorious over Satan's claim to us.

Jesus is the light. He is the one who overcomes the darkness. The lights in my life came back on, but Satan wasn't finished yet with his assault. Oh no, he wasn't. As long as I am on this earth, he will always come after me with something. Yes, he will. He proves it over and over. He came at me in the darkness of grief. He came at me through my mirror. He came at me in the gushing, swirling water of grief that was trying to drown me. He is still coming at me with various things. He doesn't like it that I can be made whiter than snow. He likes for me to be in the darkness with him. I have a choice to fight him or join him. I choose to fight my way through, knowing that God had the victory over all darkness at the cross.

I learned a powerful lesson. We live in a spiritual war zone. War is hard, and it is ever so ugly. However, we are in it whether we like it or not. When we are down at our lowest point, Satan will attack even harder. When our defenses are down, he will throw huge bombs at us. He wants to win the war in our souls. All I needed to do was to remind myself that Jesus has already won the war. It was up to me to keep getting up in the war zone and going back into the battle.

MY DREAM

Abrupt change is absolutely overwhelming and consuming. It seemed impossible not to have any contact at all with Jeremy. I felt that I just had to find a way to communicate with him. For the first month, I wrote him a letter every day. I have always liked to write. It is a help to me to put my thoughts on paper, so I kept the letters in a notebook. This especially helped because I could go back anytime and read them when I needed to feel close to him. I asked the angels to deliver these letters to him by way of spiritual messaging, and I felt confident that they did. I know in my heart that they treated each one with the utmost respect, being letters from a mother to her son. God knows my every thought, and I knew He could share my thoughts with Jeremy. It helped my sword-filled heart to think I could continue giving Jeremy something. I bought a tiny angel, who was sitting down reading a book. I placed it on the windowsill over my kitchen sink. It reminded me that he was receiving my letters. This was one way of sharing my emotions and thoughts with him. It was one way to feel that he was not cut off from me.

I talked to him too. It only made sense that I could talk to him, and he would listen. I thought of it in this way: I love Jesus. I cannot reach out and touch Him. I can't look at Him either, because He is in the spirit world. However, I know that He hears me and communicates with me in the spirit. God had assured me that Jeremy was with Him and he was okay. Jeremy had already spoken to me at the funeral home. I heard him in my spirit, so I knew that we could continue communicating in this way. This is communion from earth to heaven with the Holy Spirit in charge.

It was one month to the day that I received another blessed assurance from the Father. He allowed me to see Jeremy in a dream. It is very difficult for me to describe what I saw, but I wrote it down at the time as best I could.

I saw him from the waist up. He had on the same shirt that we buried him in. His features looked the same, except there was a difference that can only be described as glory, glory, glory! There was a beauty about him that we do not have in this world. His look was marked by wisdom, maturity, peace, happiness, contentment, love, gentleness, understanding, strength, compassion, truth, youth, beauty, and glory. All of these qualities were transparent in him. He was gorgeous and glorious! He was communicating all of these things to me without saying a word. Not one word. I was awestruck. I was also struck by his beautiful smile that was shining with grace and complete joy.

As I looked at him, marveling in this wondrous sight, there was one of those qualities that he seemed to be holding out to me and wanting to draw my attention to. It stood out from all the others and seemed to be a gift he wanted to give me. It was the quality of *understanding*. He wanted me to know that now he understands everything! Wow, oh, wow! And everything is okay! He knew what I needed at that time. Oh, what great peace this gave me because I knew I didn't understand why all of this had happened!

I woke up thinking about what the apostle Paul said when he was trying to explain the understanding that we as humans have. He said it is very limited. He compared it to looking into a poor mirror to see. The poor mirror is blurry and hazy, and we can't see God's ways as God sees and knows them (1 Corinthians 13:12).

There is only one way for us to have complete understanding, and that is after we have crossed the bridge from this world to the next. Then we will be with God and will be made perfect and complete. It is *then* that we will understand everything. And then I thought, *What about John the Baptist?* Well, what did that mean, and why did that question come to my mind? God is always teaching me. I realized God had sent that question to me. He wanted me to ponder. I started thinking about the blood relationship of Jesus and John. They were cousins because their mothers were cousins. They were blood related, and John knew that Jesus was the Messiah, the Son of God. John knew this when he was in his mother's womb, and Jesus was in His mother's womb, and the two mothers got together! Isn't that astounding? Even so, John admitted his limited understanding of everything. He knew he didn't understand everything. He just knew that God's spirit was upon Jesus without measure or limit. He knew he was the forerunner of Jesus to let people know that Jesus was coming, and he proclaimed that all who trust in Jesus to save them will live forever and ever. John had faith in Jesus and knew that Jesus was the *way to* understanding when our physical lives have been completed. John was a great man, and he helped prepare the way for the Messiah, but his understanding was limited because he was only human. We are definitely limited in our understanding here on earth. That is okay because we have our faith to carry us through until we enter His glory and receive complete understanding.

My limited understanding was okay. God wanted me to know that this was a fact of earthly life. There was no way we could understand. This is normal, and this is okay. Don't worry about it and don't try to understand it. The time would come when we would understand. The time will come when we will be made perfect and complete, but until then, we are to trust and have faith to keep going.

> Now we see but a poor reflection as in a mirror;
> then we shall see face to face.
> Now I know in part;
> then I shall know fully, even as I am fully known.
> —1 Corinthians 13:12 (NIV)

MY HEART SHATTERS

I feel it is only right that I share the physical suffering of our separation from Jeremy with you. We cannot overlook, neglect, or deny our physical bodies (we live in them), which includes the mental and emotional suffering that accompanies the death of loved ones. The road of grief is a painful journey that must be traveled in order to get to the road of healing. It is better to get up and travel it than to sit in it and never get out of it. King David had a lot of grief. Even though he was blessed and loved by God, David had loads of grief in his life. But he knew where to go with his grief, so he poured it out like water to his God whom he loved with all his heart, mind, and soul. The Psalms are full of his grieving, venting, loving, praising, requests, heartfelt messages of love, fear, guilt, sadness, and anger, his thoughts, emotions, and the guts of his soul. King David knew to pour out everything in his life to God. David asked God to deal well with him because his heart was wounded within him. It is amazing how that muscle within us that pumps out life-giving blood can hurt and feel like it is breaking. After the sword of death had been plunged into the center of my heart and soul, twisted, then pushed as far in as it could go, my heart cracked. This did not eliminate that dagger in it though. It was still hanging there and was driven so deep that at times I felt I could hardly breathe. And then when the shock of numbness wore off, my heart felt as if it had shattered into tiny, tiny pieces.

As time went on and daily life continued, it was up to me to pick up each tiny shattered piece from my heart, so that I could put all of them back together like a puzzle and create my heart again. It was my responsibility. Each piece I touched caused soul-penetrating, gut-wrenching pain that seared through me like a sharp knife. I had to learn how to live all over again. It couldn't be done without facing the pain. Ignoring the pain would not bring healing, trying to escape from the pain would not bring healing, and denying it would not bring healing.

I could only deal with a little at a time. Sometimes I had to wait for the right time to pick up a piece, and the right time was when I felt that I had the strength to do it. As I have said before, grief was such hard work. I had to apply the fruit of the Spirit to my own self. Yes, I did.

I had to learn to be patient, gentle, kind, and loving to myself. It was then that I had a moment of truth that clicked within me. Learning to apply these fruits to myself, I was learning more how to apply them to others. It was becoming ingrained in me. It was becoming a way of life. *Love your neighbor as you love yourself* became an eye-opening experience.

Denial was very hard to overcome because reality would come and go. Billy and I waited for Jeremy to come home. We could almost hear his car pull in the driveway, and it felt as though he was just about to walk in the door. We both would feel it at the same time, and we waited with false anticipation. It would be the usual time that he always came in the door. We waited, holding our breaths, just knowing he was going to walk in that door. He didn't come. So reality would set in again. When it did, so did horrible pain.

We couldn't watch television. We couldn't listen to music. We couldn't be in a crowd. Our nerves just couldn't stand it. We couldn't eat. Jeremy was not sitting at the kitchen table. Bless her heart, Julie bought us a new set of dishes to help us look at different plates, and I bought new forks with blue handles just so we could eat something without the dishes and utensils being a reminder. What a kind and loving daughter we have. She was in horrible pain herself, but she wanted to help us in any way she could, so we could eat. She knew how important that was because we didn't care if we ate or not. We started eating a little at a time, sometimes with tears running down our faces, and at the same time feeling as if we were going to choke on the food.

We couldn't stand to sit in our own living room. There was the loveseat that Jeremy always sat on, so he could look out the window. We had to get rid of that furniture. We traded our couch and loveseat for a new set, just so we could sit down without it causing so much pain and we could have a little peace.

I went to the grocery. I walked down the aisles. All of Jeremy's favorite foods seemed to jump out at me. I could not seem to put anything in the shopping cart. Panic gripped me. I left the cart in the aisle many times with nothing in it and escaped out the door practically at a run. I was having panic attacks. I went home without groceries and tried it again another day.

I walked circles in my kitchen. I couldn't remember how to cook. What do I do? I didn't even know what to do first. Nothing came to my mind. Nothing made sense. It was as if my mind had been shut down. My mind was confused, blank, and tortured. I held my hands to the sides of my head and groaned in pain.

I went down the steps to the laundry room. I had to wash clothes. How do I do that? I was blank again. I started looking for Jeremy's dirty clothes. Where were they? Where were his dirty clothes? I couldn't find his dirty clothes. I felt panic inside. I was about to scream, and then ... I remembered. I sat down on the floor with the other clothes and sobbed and sobbed and sobbed. I couldn't quit. Tears were gushing out of me. I couldn't stop them if I tried. When I was finished, I was exhausted but felt some peace. God gave me rest until the next wave hit me. My heart was bleeding profusely with every movement I made, with every shard I picked up. My heart was so sick I felt like dying. Heartsickness is a very grave sickness. Nobody could do this for me, yet I knew that I was not alone.

> But you, O Sovereign Lord,
> deal well with me for your name's sake;
> out of the goodness of your love,
> deliver me.
> For I am poor and needy,
> and my heart is wounded within me.
> —Psalm 109:21–22 (NIV)

WHY?

Hadn't I studied the book of Job and received the comfort of knowing that God was still in control? Yes, I had! Then why was I being tormented by that little word *why*? Why oh why did it come and not go away? Wasn't it enough that I was dealing with loss, grief, and pain? I didn't want to be tormented like this, yet it hammered away relentlessly at my brain. There seemed to be no relief in sight. None. I was confused. How could I know that God was still in control and yet be tormented by this little word? But then again, Job experienced this very thing during his torment. He did not give up on God, yet he wrestled and wrestled with that word, *why*.

Job was in so much torment that he cursed the day he was born.

He wanted to know why he didn't die at birth!

He wanted to know why God had even let him be born!

He said his sadness and troubles weighed heavier than the sand of a thousand seashores!

He wanted to know why he still had the strength to continue to live.

He wanted to know why God had made him His target.

He wanted to know why all of these things had happened to him.

He wanted to know why he couldn't go on and die.

The whys kept coming and coming at Job, and he let the poisonous venom out. God listened. I know He listened because He answered Job!

It was 2:00 a.m. as I lay flat on my stomach on the living room floor, crying out to God.

"Why? Why? Why?"

I was pounding the floor with my fist and crying, sobbing out to God.

"Oh, God," I cried. "I have loved you so much and believed in you since I was ten years old. I know you keep the sun in the sky and tell it when to move. You hold the moon and stars in place. You send your angels to watch over us. You answer my prayers. I know you love me.

"Where were you that night?

"Kids do all kinds of crazy things and somehow live to tell about them. I have heard men's stories of their wildness and how they somehow escaped death.

"Where was Jeremy's guardian angel that night?

"Why didn't we know about the field party?

"Why did Amanda have to die?

"Why did Jeremy have to die?

"Why did Joe have to get hurt?

"Oh, *why*?"

Like Job, I was walking through the fires. I was burning, burning, burning and on fire with it. It wouldn't go away. I had to travel on hot coals of fire to get to the other side of why. I had to keep going. I knew if I stayed on this side of why, I would become a bitter, angry woman. The why was like kindling adding fire to the anger of my grief. I kept most of this to myself. I knew that no human being on earth held the answers to the why. Oh, there might be some who would try to give me answers, but I knew it wouldn't work. I didn't want anybody's answers! I knew there were no answers. I was also afraid that if I voiced what I was going through, someone would think I was blaming God, and I wasn't. I just had to get it out of me as Job did. It was the walk I was taking that counted, not the talk I was doing. I had to make this journey by myself. My spirit was in turmoil.

We know who was after me to shatter my faith in God. He was out to break Job down completely so he would lose faith in Almighty God. We know that Satan is the father of turmoil and torment. Satan was after me and was doing all he could to pull me down further and further.

It is God who works all things together for good to them who love Him (Romans 8:28). It was in the process of working my way through the whys that I found peace. I could not go around the questions. I had to plow and push through them. Of course, Satan wanted me to stay in them. If I stayed there, he knew he had control of me. It was a very painful process, but it was also a cleansing process. And it was such hard work. I was there in the whys for several weeks, and as I worked through them and got to the other side of them, the answers didn't matter at all anymore.

Letting it all out was healing. I had to get it out before it festered into bigger problems. That's what Job was trying to do when he was asking all those questions in the presence of his friends. He was getting it out of him. He was venting, expressing, feeling, and pushing through the pain and anguish. It was his friends who couldn't handle it and tried to fix it with their own thoughts and feelings about the situation. Nobody can fix these things for us. We have to work through them ourselves.

God was big enough to handle my little pounding fists. He knew the love I carried for Him. It was not a matter of blame; it was a matter of shouting out my emotions to the One I loved. It was a matter of letting Him know the extent of my sorrow. He already knew, of course, but it was me being honest in my feelings. It was for me, not for Him. It was me not trying to hide these emotions from Him (as if I could) but giving them to Him. It was for my emotional health and sanity.

Satan did not win with his torture chamber that he had placed in my soul. He was defeated and thrown out during the fight. It was spiritual warfare big-time. I fought my way through because I did not want to stay there in this place of torment. But I did not fight alone. I couldn't fight alone. It was bigger than me. God was right by my side, even though I couldn't feel Him. We fought together until the feelings were spent and ready to leave. I did not get answers, but I got something far better than answers. I received peace that passes all understanding.

King David also went through a time in his life of asking why. He wanted to know why God had forsaken him. He wanted to know why God was so far from saving him from his enemies. He wanted to know why God was so far from his cries of agony. He wanted to know why God was not answering him (Psalm 22:1–2). However, King David did not give up on God. He never gave up. He poured out everything to God, and God never left him. It wasn't long until King David wrote the twenty-third psalm, saying, "Even though I walk through the valley of the shadow of death, I will fear no evil, for you are with me; your rod and your staff, they comfort me" (Psalm 23:4 NIV).

God knows every time a sparrow falls. He is all knowing, all-powerful. He knows exactly what we are going through. He knew His own Son would feel forsaken by Him, but He gave His Son anyway.

The Bible says Jesus felt forsaken while he hung on the cross, and He asked God *why* (Matthew 27:46).

"Why?"

It is human. It is in the heart of emotions. It is in the feelings of abandonment, in the feelings of being totally alone in grief, in the feelings of being in the valley of the shadow of death. Jesus didn't stay in His forsaken state. He cried out to His own Father about it, and then He went on to the end. That is what He said: "It is finished." He accomplished what He came to earth to do. This pain was the beginning of the unending joy to come. Yes, it was.

SIDE STREETS AND DETOURS

I have already introduced you to the enemy called the whys that attacked me during my grief. It was the first of many other kinds of torturous attacks. Jeremy hadn't been gone very long when I found myself on "if only" street, and "if only" happens to be a dead end street, just as the whys are.

Even though "if only" led nowhere, it had a great purpose and mission. Its mission was to destroy me. I didn't go out looking for this street! No, I didn't! It just continually appeared, bearing a huge "if only" sign at the entrance. Actually, the sign was so big there was no way I could miss the entrance. It beckoned me, it lured me, it trapped me, and it didn't even care. Its mission was so totally simple. Yet, as it surrounded me, I found it difficult to recognize it and see what it stood for. I wallowed in it while its torturous tentacles wrapped themselves around me. I felt like I was in a horrible pit that clutched and screamed at me. I held my stomach and cried: "Oh, Jeremy, if only … or if only …" The lists were long, and they kept coming at me.

The "if onlys" worked diligently to keep me, and they showed no mercy toward me. I felt as if I was running in circles. I felt too weak to fight back in trying to get out of this place. That is why I needed people to keep praying for me, and they did. I know they did, or I would not have gotten out.

The "if onlys" tortured me, and I ran, but I only managed to run into a sister of this monster, and of course, it was the one I was so familiar with, called "Why?"

What?

Oh no, not that again!

Why couldn't I get rid of "Why?" I thought God had helped me conquer it. I knew He did. But the whys slinked back in. They had just waited for another day to sneak back in when they knew I was weak and vulnerable, caused by the "if onlys." The demons of the whys were everywhere. They followed me, chanting their insane song of "Why, why, why?" They whined. They dripped all over me as I tried to run, and then I felt my foot slipping into something soft and slippery. I lost my footing. I was sinking, and I didn't have the energy to pull out of it. I was in something dark and nasty. I couldn't recognize where I was. It was a big pothole in the street of "if only!" The whys had chased me into it! This pothole had grabbing fingers. All of these streets of torment have these deep potholes. What were they?

And then I knew.

These were self-pity holes! They were slimy, smelly, and nasty. Getting out of one felt impossible, yet this feeling was not truth. Feelings can be liars. Thoughts can be liars, and these liars were hard to filter through my mind and heart. I had to hang onto the truth, and the truth was that with God by my side, all things were possible! I could get out of these streets and potholes. I just knew I could. I would not give in to these enemies! I had to use everything within me to fight back. It was not easy because they did not give up without a battle. I was hanging on by my fingertips.

Self-pity was a deep hole that absolutely wanted to swallow me up and eat me alive. It was slimy and got all over me, making it difficult to climb up and get out of it. When I couldn't get out of it, it veered off fast and took me with it, popping me up into another street whose name was depression. Now I was engulfed with self-pity and was depressed. Depression had many disguises, and by now I was so sick that I didn't even recognize that I was there. I even denied that depression had a hold on me. I felt lifeless. I had no energy. I felt worthless and eaten up with despair. I felt very sick, and it felt as if my life's blood had been sucked right out of me. My energy level was hitting zero.

I knew the devil was after my very soul, and I was no match for him by myself. Eve wasn't either. I knew I must fight these enemies, but I simply could not do it by myself. Others were praying for me to find my way out. This gave me strength. I weakly grabbed my shield of faith and held it in front of me. I held it unsteadily, but slowly I raised it up high, and the fight was on again. I was not going down without a fight! I had not been defeated yet.

I turned up my light. I needed light to see how to get out of these tricky, nasty places. I knew the Word of God was my light.

"Your word is a lamp to my feet and a light for my path" (Psalm 119:105 NIV).

I started searching in the Word. I put on the rest of God's armor. Ephesians 6:10–28 (NIV) advises:

> Finally, be strong in the Lord and in His mighty power. Put on the full armor of God so that you can take your stand against the devil's schemes. For our struggle is not against flesh and blood, but against the rulers, against the authorities, against the powers of this dark world and against the spiritual forces of evil in the heavenly realms. Therefore put on the full armor of God, so that when the day of evil comes, you may be able to stand your ground, and after you have done everything, to stand. Stand firm then, with the belt of truth buckled around your waist, with the breastplate of righteousness in place, and with your feet fitted with the readiness that comes from the gospel of peace. In addition to all this, take up the shield of faith, with which you can extinguish all the flaming arrows of the evil one. Take the helmet of salvation and the sword of the Spirit, which is the word of God. And pray in the Spirit on all occasions with all kinds of prayers and requests. With this in mind, be alert and always keep on praying for all the saints.

I had on my armor, and I knew where to go. I was searching for the narrow road that leads to home with God and away from this devil torment.

Where is the hidden small gate that will lead me out of these nasty places? "Enter through the narrow gate. For wide is the gate and broad is the road that leads to destruction, and many enter through it. But small is the gate and narrow the road that leads to life, and only a few find it" (Matthew 7:13 NIV).

I was familiar with the wide gates. They were everywhere. There was no use pretending that they weren't there. They seemed to have neon signs that beckoned and then consumed me when I entered. They were real, and I had to work hard to escape. They attacked my feelings and my thoughts. They wreaked havoc with my emotions, and they made me physically ill.

God had provided a way for me to get out, but the narrow gate was hidden, so I knew I must find it. The scriptures had given me an action plan. I started to proceed.

I knew the only way to find the hidden small gate was to use the sword, which is the Word of God. I needed to memorize the Word and put those words of truth around my waist like a belt and wear them. This is my gut area. I had to listen to my gut, my instinct, the real me, my soul who wants to listen to and follow the Word of God.

I needed to do the right things that come from my heart, which is the breastplate of righteousness. I needed to guard my heart and make sure my heart was putting God first. This meant striving to do the things that were right in God's sight.

I needed to share the gospel of peace with others but first remind myself of it. This involved teaching a class at church every Sunday morning. This included telling others about how God was leading me through my grief and how I knew He was still in control. This was about my testimony of God's mercy, grace, and abundant love.

I needed to carry my shield of faith always to keep the darts of Satan's side streets and detours from penetrating my soul. He was going to come after me with nasty remarks in my head that would bring me down if I didn't hold out my shield of faith to distinguish them. My shield of faith was stronger than Satan when I used it because God lives in me, and He is greater than anything Satan can do to me. I had to remember the importance of the shield of faith and not waver.

I needed to put on the helmet of salvation, which said Jeremy was saved and so am I. Everything is okay!

I needed to keep praying to my Father in heaven for deliverance from the evil one, and I also needed to pray for others.

We are in God's army. We are soldiers. Soldiers have each other's backs. Other people helped. Either I called them or God sent them to help support me. They helped to hold me up on the days that I was too sick to support myself by myself. On my stronger days, I searched for the narrow road.

I knew that those wide gates of "if only" and "why" with their horrible potholes of self-pity and depression would only lead to the destruction of myself. They were Satan's roads. His roads are so big, so wide, and so loud. They blared, beckoning me, tempting me, making me feel I had no choice. I couldn't miss them. I could not pretend they didn't exist as the devil wanted me to. To deny them would put me right into his hands to do as he pleased with me. I couldn't shove them out of the way either. I couldn't give in to them even though at times it seemed I wanted to. That was the devil tempting me to stay there and ruin my life. I had to stay alert, as the Bible says to do. I did have a choice! Even though they were dead-end streets, I plowed through them. I had to so I could get to the other side of them and escape. I got to the other side, slammed their doors shut, and breathed again. I had found the narrow gate!

God was with me in these horrible places during my grief. I cannot act as if these places do not exist. I am not above them. I am not untouched by them. No one is. I am human. We all are human. Job was not untouched by these either. I felt so kindred to Job again. He is my special, special friend. As Job was, I was in this world where these horrible places exist. I was luckier than Job though. There was not one person who scolded me for being in these places as his friends did to him. Praise the Lord! It would only have driven me further in. I needed support, love, encouragement, prayers, and the presence of others around me, and I had all of that. I needed God's army of armed soldiers, and I had them. I praise God for all those gifts He gave me through others who are His saints.

I know it was and is a part of grief that I had to endure. If I had not worked my way through them, I would still be stuck in them, but it did take years of off-and-on battle with the enemy. Each time I fought my way out, I felt freedom and light. Satan fought hard to keep me in the horrible pits, but God worked with me to find my way out. However, I know that

I must be careful, always careful, because to let my guard down, not to have my armor on, not to be alert can have devastating results of being sucked back in.

I must continually stay on God's street, the narrow one that leads home. God's road is small, quiet, and peaceful, and I must search for it faithfully and fight for it. It is one continuous road that meanders through life. It is totally straight because it is truth. When I find truth, I have found the straight and narrow way. The truth comes from God. God gives perfect peace to those whose minds stay on Him and trust Him (Isaiah 26:3–4).

The truth brings hope and sunshine and light.

Satan is a liar and a betrayer. He cannot be trusted. Torment comes from him. It is his job! It is the job he took on because he wanted it. He loves his job. And he is good at it! I must recognize his side roads, his detours that he plants ever so cleverly. If I am being tormented, I have entered one of his streets, which are numerous. Once I enter, he bombards without mercy. He thoroughly enjoys bombarding the grieving, but Jesus has made a way for us to find peace.

In John 14:27, Jesus told His disciples that He was leaving His own peace to them. They had many trials and hardships after He left. But He left His peace with them and told them not to be afraid or troubled.

This peace is not of this world. It is from heaven. It is real. It comes in the midst of the storm. It comes during the fight. It comes at last. My battles were not over, but I had peace after every battle.

> Peace I leave with you; my peace I give you.
> I do not give to you as the world gives.
> Do not let your hearts be troubled
> and do not be afraid.
> —John 14:27 (NIV)

GUILT

I had traveled through the hot coals of the whys and the "if onlys" and finally got relief when along came another demon that tried to possess me. Horrifying guilt set in. It was not guilt that I could get away from, and it was not guilt that I could confess, repent, and purge out of me. I'm talking huge, heavy masses of guilt. It was so massive I couldn't stand it. It overwhelmed me. It consumed me and tormented me relentlessly. I felt like such a bad mother. Mothers are supposed to take care of their children. That is what we do, and I felt that I had failed. It was awful. I tried expressing my guilt to my loved ones, and it hurt them so to see me suffer like this. They would say things like, "Rhonda, you know you were a good mother."

It didn't help. It didn't help at all. At the time, it didn't even make sense to me, and most of all, it didn't seem true. I knew I needed some extra help with this. Our minister, Scott, and his family had moved away to minister to a church in another state. We were currently without a minister. I grew up going to a church in Chaplin. Billy and I went there, taking Julie and Jeremy for many years before we joined a church in Bloomfield where we lived. I knew I had to have help. The Lord led me to call a minister that we used to have at the church in Chaplin. Most everybody called him Fella. I knew where he and his family had moved since leaving Chaplin, and since it was in a town not too far away from our town, I called and asked him if he would come and help me.

I knew in my heart that the Lord had led me to call him. I was so right. Fella came right away, and I poured out the guilty feelings that were controlling me. These feelings and thoughts of guilt had their tentacles wrapped tight around me and refused to let go. I was in bondage.

He listened carefully until I was finished. Then he said something that I could call my truth, and it helped tremendously.

He said, "Rhonda, you are right, you weren't a perfect mother. In fact, there aren't any perfect mothers. No one is perfect, but the truth is you did more things right than you did wrong."

That was it! That felt right! I felt a measurable amount of relief instantly. That's the way truth is. Truth sets us free. It set me free from the awful, all-consuming guilt that had me paralyzed and tormented. With that torment on me, I had not even been able to think of one good thing I had done for Jeremy as his mother. However, when he said, "You did more things right than you did wrong," it freed me from the guilt that had entered me to destroy me. The truth set me free!

I was so thankful for Fella's wonderful words that were like a healing balm to my troubled soul. I was so much better until Satan snatched that peace out from under me. You see, Satan didn't like it that I had been set free from the false guilt that he had put on me. He decided to use a different approach of attack. It brings so many emotions to me right now as I tell what happened.

I was sitting in my usual spot having my coffee and alone time with God early on a Sunday morning. All of a sudden, I looked up. I didn't see a thing, but I felt something huge and awful beside me. It felt as if there was a huge dump truck backing up to my side. It slowly started raising the back of the truck up while at the same time it was unloading a truckload of guilt all over me. It was smothering me, and I felt I couldn't breathe. I started choking with this cumbersome guilt. I took off running to the bathroom as quickly as I could, and I slammed the door behind me. I got on my knees in front of the commode and bent over it. I just knew I was going to be sick, or it would choke me to death.

The tears started flowing hard and fast as I was coughing and choking.

I cried, "Oh, Jeremy, there are things I did I wish I hadn't done." I gasped for air between the sobbing and said, "There are things I didn't do I wish I had done."

Then I said, "And there are things I would do differently now if I could.

"Oh, Jeremy, please forgive me. Please, please forgive me!" I begged.

I had poured it all out and was still choking and sobbing when I heard something. It was so powerful that I quieted down immediately.

Jeremy's spirit was in the bathroom with me! I felt his presence, and he spoke back to me!

He said, "Mom, I wasn't perfect either. There are things I did I wish I hadn't done. There are things I didn't do that I wish I had done. There are things I would do differently now if I could."

Then he said, "Mom, it's *okay*."

He said the same things back to me that I had said to him!

I sat up in total astonishment!

In that instant, the guilt was cleared away.

It was gone.

Jeremy said it was okay! I cried more tears than ever, only this time they were tears of joy.

Satan had unloaded that truckload of guilt on me, hoping that I would stay in guilt all my life. He knew this guilt would paralyze me and suck the life out of me, and that was his aim for me. He wanted me to stay in bondage and torment. When he poured that guilt all over me, it was too much for me to bear, and I couldn't get it off by myself. God knew this and sent my Jeremy to take it off me. He wasted no time in defeating Satan's evil attempt at giving me a life of complete torment for the rest of my days on this earth.

I praise God Almighty for His wondrous love. He came like the wind and relieved me of the horrendous guilt Satan had put on me. He set me free with His truth.

THE NEWSPAPER

I counted the pages. There were forty of them that had something written about Jeremy and Amanda starting on May 19, 1996, and the last article being written on June 2, 1997. The last article was not about them but about another young man who had been killed while attending a field party. However, in the same article, they included Amanda and Jeremy's story. This was entirely unnecessary because the community was still healing from it and certainly did not need to be reminded about it. I was working at school at the time as an instructional assistant in kindergarten. Lizzie, the school secretary, had gotten the paper that morning and saw the article. She came and brought me out of class to warn me, to protect me, to let me know about it so I wouldn't be knocked off my feet if I saw it before I got home. She cared about me and wanted to soften the blow. It was entirely unnecessary to bring all that back up in the paper. I was hit in the gut really hard for the family of this young man because I knew the pain and agony ahead for his parents as they grieved for their son. I knew the pain ahead for all his family members and his friends. Jeremy knew this young man, and that was hard too. All of that pain was enough without them bringing up our loss along with it. Oh, what were they thinking to do this? I appreciated Lizzie's kindness and thoughtfulness in warning me ahead of time and letting me get prepared. We were all like family at that school. We supported each other. It was a marvelous gift to have the love and respect for each other that we had in our workplace.

Road Trip: Jesus, Jeremy and Me

My opinion is that the newspaper was definitely heartless about our tragedies, especially in the weeks after the tragedies. Perhaps I felt this way because my child was the topic, and he was dead. That makes sense to me. My emotions were ugly raw when I was reading those articles. As I have said before, words have great power. They have the power to soothe and help heal, or words can be dangerous weapons that can cut like a two-edged sword. Their words were like dumping a load of salt into that open, gaping wound in my shattered heart and then rubbing that salt in very hard.

The accident happened at 2:30 in the morning of May 19, 1996. The paper immediately had all the answers, including all the whys and the hows. It was all cut and dried. How could it be all summed up when we hadn't even had a chance to put anything together for a picture of what happened? It didn't end there in that edition. They kept the story going for a long time. Hate and bitterness toward the paper started growing in my heart. Two children were dead, and yet the writers felt they had to send more messages out to parents of teenagers and to teenagers themselves. I was sickened in my soul.

Many people had opinions and felt that they had to express them. Some blamed the field party, some blamed people who sell alcohol to minors, and others blamed teens themselves. Some blamed the schools, the community, a lack of role models, anything and everything they could think of. In fact, it became a heated debate over playing the blame game. This tragedy had hit our community hard, and people everywhere were hurting and angry. There were articles, interviews, and editorials, whatever they could think of to keep this going. They were selling papers.

The parents of Jeremy and Amanda were blamed. Jeremy was blamed. The people who gave permission for the field party to be held at the park were blamed. I actually felt that I was on the floor and people were hurling stones at me to finish killing me. That is how bad it was to me.

They had their turn to speak, and now it is my turn. I have kept silent all these years, but not anymore. I started to not put this in this book, but it was a part of my pain; it was a part of my story, so here goes.

Again I called Fella.

"Help me, please," I said.

I just had to have help. The Lord knew who was best to give me that help. God bless that man. He came, and oh, yes, he helped me. I showed him the articles and explained the bad feelings that were growing in my heart. He read some of them that were hurtful to our family and friends, and you know what? He became angry too. He cared about all of us, and this hurt him also. We discussed some of the writings. He listened to me intently as I shared my thoughts and feelings of what I was experiencing, and how it was affecting me. He sympathized with me. He comforted me. And then he took all this to the Lord. He prayed for me. He prayed that God would deliver me from this horrible stuff that was brewing in me toward the newspaper and the writers. It worked. I do not carry bitterness in my heart. I'm just telling my story.

As Jeremy's parents, we were not the only ones hurting from all of this. Julie and Brian were hurting. Jeremy's entire extended family and friends were suffering too and didn't know what to do about it. Amanda's parents, her sisters and brothers, her extended families and friends were suffering the same as we were. It was awful.

There were many people who were helping us with this. They cared deeply that we were being blasted by the paper, and they shielded us as much as possible. I thank them from the bottom of my heart for their kindness and compassion.

As for me, it left deep, deep scars. I lost trust in the media at that point in my life. I needed to learn that this happens to other people all the time. I hadn't stopped to think about it before. I do believe in free press and freedom of speech, so what can I say? Well, because of that very thing, I can have my say, too. I can express the fact that even now, I do not like to read the paper. Even though I do not have bitterness toward it, I do not care about it. I do not have the desire to read it. They took away my joy of reading the paper. My desire to read it was killed when Jeremy was killed, and the paper used it to their advantage. I can only speak my opinion and my heart.

Now, I would also say there were some very good things in there. I thank them for that. We appreciated all the love of those who gave their time and effort to write good things about Jeremy and Amanda. I am not saying it was all bad. It just so happens that for me, the bad seemed to outweigh the good. To me, the most horrifying of all was running an article about how a seventeen-year-old boy felt when he was dead and in his casket. The timing of running this article was heartless to the families of Jeremy and Amanda. Maybe there could have been a little more empathy if they had, in their minds, inserted their own child's name. Maybe it would have helped to put their own child's name in that article when it said the seventeen-year-old boy was talking about his life as they were putting him into his casket. Maybe there would have been more sympathy toward those of us who were picking out caskets and picking out gravesites for our children.

What happened to compassion? I was infuriated and sickened by this total lack of respect to us, the grieving families.

Do I sound angry? Well, of course I do! It still stirs me up because it was not right. I can have righteous indignation. I can have righteous anger when something is not right and good. Now that I have experienced this, God has taken this bad stuff and worked it together for good for me. I now understand and have compassion for people who are slaughtered by the press. I never thought about it before, but my heart goes out to them now, and I pray for those who have to endure this when their worlds fall apart. It happens all the time to the unfortunate ones left behind in a tragedy that really strikes the interest of the public media. And now every time I see sensationalism used on TV, at the newsstands, or in magazines (which is a lot), it sickens me. Now I have experienced being on that side of the fence.

I have worked hard at letting this go with the Lord's help. I think about the people who worked at the paper at that time, and I do have compassion for them. Perhaps they did not know how to handle such great pain, turmoil, and debate in the community. I also want to be forgiven of my sins (which are many); therefore, I must forgive the paper and its writers. That's what Jesus says we have to do. I have told the facts. This was a part of my story. I can't change anything about what happened during this time. It is all written in my heart and a part of me. I do have the choice over whether or not to let it go. It is my desire to forgive and let it go. It does take time for wounds and nerves to heal, and I have come a long way toward that healing. What happens to us emotionally is in our physical bodies as well and causes physical, mental, emotional and health problems. I used to feel as if I was physically choking every time I saw a paper. I don't feel that anymore, and in all honesty, I don't think about it very much. I have had a lot of healing. I am only writing this because it is part of my story. Maybe someday I will be interested in the paper again. If the interest doesn't come, I am all right with that too. It is just like getting burned on a wood stove. The burn may heal, but it may leave a scar, and that scar will keep me from getting that close to the stove again. I will be cautious. I will be careful. I will be particular about what I read.

Sometime during that time, Billy and I had a piece put in the paper that I had written about our son. It went in the back of the paper where memories can be included for a fee.

This is the memory that I wrote:

> NEVER AGAIN … … … will we hear Jeremy say, "Hey Mom, what's for supper?"
>
> Do you have time to iron this shirt real quick? Dad, if you're going to Walmart, will you get me some oil?
>
> Do either of you have any quarters? I want to wash my car.
>
> ARE WE OUT OF KETCHUP?!
>
> NEVER AGAIN … … will he weed-eat, take out the trash, wash his jeans,
>
> or make macaroni & cheese, scrambled eggs or grilled cheese.
>
> Our patio table that he was going to sand and paint will have to wait until we have the heart to do it.
>
> NEVER AGAIN … … … will he eat supper with us, sit on our bed and talk to us, clean mud up off the floor that he tracked in, sit with us in church, remind us not to talk about people because you aren't supposed to, or go out to see his friends.
>
> His room is empty, his door is shut, his car is gone, and the house is silent.
>
> Our hearts are broken.

All of us make mistakes, miss the mark, sometimes do it wrong. We must forgive if we want God to forgive us. I forgive the newspaper. I forgive the writers. I know it was a bad time for everyone.

> For if you forgive men
> when they sin against you,
> your Heavenly Father
> will also forgive you.
> But if you do not forgive men their sins,
> your Father will not forgive your sins.
> —Matthew 6:14–15 (NIV)

30
DRIVEN TO THE CEMETERY

I had a deep desire in me to go to the cemetery. It would not go away. It goaded me, drove me, and even seemed to push me to go to Jeremy's grave. It didn't matter what I was doing when this came over me; I would stop, get in the car, and just go. The cemetery was just about five miles away, so it didn't take long to get there. When I got there, I felt that I couldn't get close enough to him. What I wanted to do was lie right down on top of his grave with my face buried against his face.

I did not understand these strong feelings. It was like a craving, but that wasn't the only reason I didn't understand it. You see, I never was one to want to go to the cemetery. I had never had a desire to go there. It had never made any sense to me because I knew the person's spirit was not there. So, what was going on here? Why did I have this drive inside of me? I didn't know what this drive was trying to tell me.

I called Fella again. "Please come and help me," I pleaded.

He is a patient and loving man of God. He came. I told him about this drive that I had to go to the cemetery. I explained that I didn't understand it, and I couldn't seem to control it. Fella was able to explain it to me in such a way that spoke truth to my spirit. Having this experience, I can say that I have learned more about the power of truth. What I learned is that truth can help me with self-control, anxiety, confusion, and internal turmoil. Truth set me free from torment. This truth did not take away my desire to go to the cemetery at that time. Oh no, it didn't, but it helped me to understand the desire and accept it until I could heal. Those things brought peace—wonderful peace. The other way truth helped me was the knowing that I didn't have to fight these feelings now that I understood them. There was truth in these feelings, and I had to nourish this truth in me. Fighting them was exhausting and getting me nowhere. Knowledge, understanding, and acceptance of these feelings were keys to my healing. Now I knew what to do. I would nurture these feelings until that part of my grief was gone. I would take care of them. I did not know this before. Now I could go to the cemetery in peace without driving myself crazy by asking questions. I could go in peace without confusion in my thinking. I could go in peace, cherishing these feelings and loving this part of me. I could go to the cemetery without turmoil rolling inside me like a big ball with no place to go. Yes, Fella was one of those Godsends that helped me with my healing. He explained it to me like this:

He told me that Jeremy's grave held the part of Jeremy that Billy and I had created together. Even though Jeremy's spirit was not there, his physical body was. His physical body came from my body, and it is a part of both Billy and me. That is why I felt as though I couldn't get close enough. Part of me was in that ground!

I knew the truth when I heard it! It rang so true to me! Truth brings peace, which is a fruit of the Holy Spirit. This truth gave me peace in the going to and coming from the cemetery. I went as often as I needed to, for as long as I needed to, and I was not tormented any longer by the drive to go there. I acknowledged it. I accepted it. I respected it. It took a long time, but as time went by, the intense desire disappeared as I cherished it and loved it as the healing tool that it was.

Then something else set in. I went through a period of time when anger would come and go when I got to the cemetery. I knew that anger was a part of grief, and I felt it deeply at different times, but why at the cemetery? I was really mad at Jeremy. Does that make any sense? Not to me! Why would I be mad at him? And then the answer came.

I was mad at him for leaving me!

Well, where did that come from?

I knew he did not leave me on purpose, so why be mad at him? This was totally unreasonable, but it felt so real. Sometimes when I was at the cemetery, I wanted to kick his headstone as hard as I could. I didn't, of course, because I had the sense to know it could possibly break my foot. I didn't want a broken foot!

I learned that anger is not always reasonable, but that doesn't make any difference with its presence. It was there to stay and refused to go away. This was about me. Part of me was in that ground, and I didn't like it one bit! These were my feelings of being abandoned by my own child whom I loved so much in this world. Children are not supposed to die before parents! He had gone on before me and without me! You know how as parents we always want to know where our children are, and if we can't find them because they have gone where they are not supposed to go, we get angry? He had gone where he wasn't supposed to go, and I was angry! He was already in the ground, and I was still living on this earth. I was mad, mad, mad! This was unreasonable anger that had to be expressed, and there were ways to deal with it. This anger in me was an emotion that needed to be acknowledged, heard, respected, and dealt with! Since my mind and my heart did not agree on this subject (my mind knew what happened, but my heart was fighting it), the anger was there to stay until I could work through it. It was important for me to let this anger out so it would not set up housekeeping in my soul. You know, there was no use in pretending it wasn't there! That would be lying to myself. My own self knew the truth, so that wouldn't help a thing! In fact, if I had denied any of my emotions during this time of grieving, it would have made me sick in my soul because lies are poison. It is the truth in all things that set me free. It still does and always will! So, when I went to the cemetery and felt those angry feelings, I would pretend in my mind that I was kicking that stone as hard as I could. I kicked, and I kicked, and I kicked as hard as I could until in my mind that stone fell and was gone. This gave vent to my anger until it dissolved itself. I wasn't mad at Jeremy any longer. The unreasonable anger was spent. I knew he didn't leave me on purpose, and through all this mental venting, I knew it in my mind, in my heart, and in my soul. I had found peace.

Fella's words were perfect to me during the time that my emotions were driving me to the cemetery and then fighting inside me at the cemetery. His words were medicine to my shattered, bleeding heart. The Lord used Fella in many ways to help me deal with my grief. The Lord used Fella because Fella let the Lord work through him.

I was very thankful and really blessed to have such medicine from the Lord.

> A man finds joy in giving an apt reply—
> and how good is a timely word!
> —Proverbs 15:23 (NIV)

SAFE FROM THE EVIL

Before the accident, we had planned to take a weekend trip to Gatlinburg, Tennessee, with Julie and Brian during the month of July. Now, everything had changed, and we weren't sure what to do. We didn't know if we were up to it or not, but we decided to give it a try.

It was very hard. I can't tell you how hard it was. We had to draw away at times to cry, to let it out, but there were good times in between. It was good to be with Julie and Brian, and after our cries, we enjoyed ourselves until the next crying spell would hit.

We were in the beautiful Smokey Mountains and had climbed to the top of Clingman's Dome. I stood there on top of that mountain searching the skies for some sign of my child or angels. I knew he was up there, and I also knew there were angels all around us. I didn't give it up. My heart was in the sky and in the hopes that I would see something with my spiritual eyes. My heart, mind, and soul were wide open in expectation when all of a sudden he jumped out at me.

When I say he, I mean Satan. Oh, yes, he really did. This is what happened.

I had already started walking back down that steep mountain, and I was walking by myself. My knees were hurting as I was going downhill, so I was taking it slow. Everyone else had gone on ahead of me, and he knew it.

When he jumped out in front of me, I stopped dead in my tracks. He came in a flash of red. He radiated evil. I had never felt so much downright evil in my entire life. This evil was all around me but mostly in front of me where he was. He was everything that I had always heard about him. I know there have been others who have experienced his presence. He is very real. Oh, yes, he is. He was thrown out of heaven because of his evilness, and he is the one who creates all the misery for us here on earth. He is invisible most of the time, but when he feels it's necessary, he makes an appearance.

He hissed at me and then snarled at me. The hissing and snarling were full of evil and contempt for me. I felt his hate toward me. He hates me so much because I love the Lord. He made me feel worthless with his attitude of disgust, total dislike, and disrespect. It was almost as if he spat it all out at once. He made it clear he despised me. His intent was to destroy the quality of my life on this earth, and he knew where to hit me the hardest. He had an announcement for me. He told me that he had my son.

Those were his exact words, "I have your son."

I did not hesitate. I came right back at him and said, "No, you don't. I know where my son is and don't you ever come to see me again!"

He vanished. He left as suddenly as he had appeared. I stood motionless. I was stunned that this had happened. I just stood there on that mountain while thinking it all through. Believe it or not, he didn't scare the living day lights out of me. I was amazed at that. My heart on that mountain was completely looking for God, for Godly things, so I was surrounded by heaven itself. This protected me from fear. God had already given me so many blessed assurances that Jeremy was with Him that I did not have any trace of doubt in my heart where Jeremy was. Satan had hoped that I would believe him instead of God. I stood up to that evil with the goodness of faith, hope, and love, but believe me I didn't do this by myself. Oh, no I didn't. He is stronger than I, but the Holy Spirit in me helped me stand up to him. Satan couldn't stand up against the Holy Spirit, and he knew it, but he tried. He always tries.

Satan had come at me in the whys. He had come at me in the "if onlys." He had come at me with depression, sorrow, self-pity, anger, confusion, bitterness, and agony. He had come at me with massive guilt. He was getting his greatest thrills, kicking and stomping on me while I was down. When we are down, he will take his boot and grind his heel on us as hard as he can. He hates us Christians with a passion. He worked really hard in all his devious pleasures against me. I was making progress toward healing, and he didn't like that—not one bit.

This time he came at me with a direct hit by appearing to me. He knew if he could scare me, if he could instill fear in me by his presence, and if he could lie to me and get away with it, he would have me by the throat. I would choke to death in his torment. If he could convince me that he had Jeremy, then life for me would be intolerable, and he knew it. That is how evil he is. He knows that in the end he is going to perish, and he wants to take as many of us with him as possible, and in the meantime persecute and torment us in the process.

In the Garden of Eden, he used the power of his words to create sin. He has not quit doing that. That is his life. He has power with his slimy words, but one of the things that will scare him off immediately is truth. When I spoke the truth, he was gone. There was nothing for him to do except to leave!

Of course this doesn't stop him from coming back. He uses countless other ways because he will not give up until my life is over. He wants me, for sure and for certain, but I know that God is greater and God lives in me.

> You, dear children, are from God
> and have overcome them,
> because the one who is in you
> is greater than the one who is in the world.
> —1 John 4:4 (NIV)

God is greater than Satan, and God lives in me! Our fight is spiritual. Satan especially wants Christians. He would like to stomp out Christianity entirely, and he works hard at it. He is against God.

In the years following this encounter I had with Satan, I studied about the temptations that Jesus went through in that wilderness. I had known about this story of Jesus's life, but I hadn't taken an in-depth look at it. Oh my! The more I studied it, the more I realized that Jesus went through extreme temptation. Satan wanted Jesus worst of all! He wanted Him more than anybody on earth. He pulled out all his artillery and started shooting his evil arrows at the Son of God, and it wasn't pretty. It was evil. This is found in Matthew 4:1–10.

He came at Jesus first of all by attacking his physical body in its weakened state from fasting. Jesus had gone without food for forty days and forty nights, and Satan knew about this. He knew how weak and hungry Jesus was, and of course, he just loves to kick and prod when the going is already rough. He specializes in these very down times. He came at Him, using what Jesus physically needed the most at that moment, which was food. He thought he could get Jesus to start using His power for His own needs. He tried to get Jesus to turn stones into bread. I can just hear him now in his yellow-bellied, slimy, lying, deceiving, voice, "Oh come on now, Jesus, you know how hungry you are; use your power for your own gain for a change! You know you *can*. You have fed lots of people before. Why not feed yourself?"

Now what would have been wrong with that? Jesus is hungry. He is physically weak. What would be wrong with Jesus using His power for taking care of Himself? He had fed other people, hadn't He? He was in the wilderness by himself. No one else was around. No one else would know. Well, Jesus knew if he gave into using His power in that way, that it would only be the beginning of Satan's temptations to do this or to do that for worldly gain. Anytime we give in the least little bit, Satan gains ground. It would be the beginning of many temptations to use His power for His own fleshly self. Jesus was not supposed to use His power for earthly gain. He could have turned those stones into bread if he had wanted to do it. In fact, He could have created a grand feast for Himself if He had wanted to! He could have brought forth riches. He could have had anything He wanted on this earth while He lived here. He could have lived in a mansion, a castle, purchased all the land He wanted, had the best chefs in the world and servants all around Him, but that wasn't His mission. He knew He had to nip this in the bud or this monster would have grounds to start digging in to take over the physical, human side of Him. Jesus knew that Satan wanted Him to sin. He wanted Him to forget about His mission.

Isn't that what he does with us? He knows our weaknesses and starts in with tempting us to do one small thing that is wrong. It sounds so good and, of course, harmless. Oh how he whispers all those little suggestions to our spirits. The list is endless, and he can make it sound like fun. He can make it sound like a feel-good moment. He knows what he is doing. He fishes for us using all kinds of bait. He dangles it in front of us like the wonderful golden carrot. We know how he operates. He comes at us all the time about something. He tries his best to gain ground in our lives for one reason: to destroy us.

Jesus refused to give in. He would not turn those stones to bread.

How many times are we admonished to just say, "No"? It is one little word that has lots of power; but if we do not ask the Lord to help us say it and stick to it, then we are whipped ... because this evil one is stronger than we are by ourselves! I know. I have experienced it many times and given in to his suggestions and wished I hadn't! I didn't know that my willpower is not enough on its own. Satan is stronger than I am. It took a long time for this to sink into my head. I have had too many consequences that prove it is true.

Jesus teaches us where the power lies in saying no to Satan. The power is the power of God. The power is in the scripture, which is the holy Word of God. This is power, power, wonder-working, miracle-working power!

"Jesus answered, 'It is written: Man does not live on bread alone, but on every word that comes from the mouth of God'" (Matthew 4:4).

Jesus knew He could turn those stones into bread. He did not have to have Satan telling Him He could do that. But Satan knows how to tempt us and break us down to do what we know we shouldn't do. It's not easy to say no, but Jesus knew He had to. The power that Jesus had was not to be used for His own conveniences. This life is temporary. The most important part of us is our everlasting souls that Jesus came to save. Jesus was keeping His priorities straight. He was keeping His eyes on His mission.

He came to feed our souls and to obey God, His Father. He told Satan that it takes more than bread for our lives.

We do not live just to eat.

There's more to us than that. We need spiritual bread most of all. That spiritual bread we need is Jesus. Jesus is our bread of life. He is our everything. He is our way to everlasting life.

And Satan was after our spiritual bread! Shame on him!

Jesus said, "I tell you the truth, he who believes has everlasting life. I am the bread of life. Your forefathers ate the manna in the desert, yet they died. But here is the bread that comes down from heaven, which a man may eat and not die. I am the living bread that came down from heaven. If anyone eats of this bread, he will live forever. This bread is my flesh, which I will give for the life of the world" (John 6:47–51 NIV).

Jesus is the bread of eternal life.

Now, Satan used the same schemes that he used all the time when he was tempting Jesus. He cannot tempt us in the same way he tempted Jesus because we don't have the power to do the things that he was tempting Jesus to do. We can't turn stones into bread. Jesus did have that power, but He refused to use it for His earthly gain. So, Satan comes at us in things we can do, and in each temptation is the lure of the flesh over the spirit. It is the lure of the earthly over the heavenly. Jesus knew if He gave into the bread thing, then Satan had a loophole to prod Him to do other things. He let the scripture do the talking for Him.

Oh well, that bread thing didn't work, but Satan did not give up. Of course not! It is not in his nature to give up so easily. If this doesn't work, go at it from another angle is his way of thinking. He took Jesus to Jerusalem to the roof of the temple and dared him to jump off. Why would he dare him to do that? He wanted him to prove that He was the Son of God. Can you believe it? Who is Jesus going to prove this to?

He wanted to instill doubt into Jesus's own mind about being the Son of God. The nerve of him! Let's see what Matthew says about it. "Then the devil took him to the holy city and had him stand on the highest point of the temple. 'If you are the Son of God,' he said, 'throw yourself down.' For it is written: 'He will command his angels concerning you, and they will lift you up in their hands, so that you will not strike your foot against a stone'" (Matthew 4:5–6 NIV).

The devil was so clever to insert that "if" you are the Son of God in there. Or so he thought! Instill doubt in ourselves is part of his game plan.

Jesus knew what he was trying to do, and He also knew the scripture that Satan quoted was true. He knew the angels would come. But did that make it right? What did Jesus use to answer this one?

"Jesus answered him, 'It is also written: Do not put the Lord your God to the test'" (Matthew 4:7 NIV).

Did Jesus have to prove to Satan who He was? No, He did not. Jesus knew who He was. He was secure in His identity. He also knew that Satan knew who He was! But the devil attacked Him on this very thing.

The devil wanted Him to doubt Himself and do something to prove who He was. This second temptation comes at us as well. It is when he makes us feel inferior inside. He can make us doubt ourselves. He can make us doubt our self-worth. He can make us doubt that we are a part of God's family. He pushes us repeatedly and in various ways to do things that are not healthy. We do these things in our efforts to try to prove who we are to ourselves and to others. This is a never-ending job, and he knows it. It is self-defeating. This keeps our focus on our fleshly egos and can never give us peace of mind about ourselves.

Satan knows scripture and uses it to back up what he is trying to get us to do. He used scripture with Jesus when he told Him that God would send angels to keep Him from harm if He would just go ahead and jump. Yes, he had the nerve to use scripture! And he still does! Don't ever put it past him. He knows how to twist scripture to use it against us and for him. He is a dirty dog. If someone is trying to get us to do something wrong and using scripture to back it up, then Satan is behind it. Satan has not changed since that day in the Garden of Eden when he coaxed Eve and then Adam into taking the forbidden fruit. He is superbly talented in mixing a little bit of truth in with a pack of lies to trap people.

Jesus knew Satan was only telling part of the scriptures. But these extreme temptations that Satan was throwing at Jesus were not easy. Oh no, they weren't. They were horrendous. He wasn't finished either.

Okay, that didn't work, so what's next? He decided to take Him to the peak of a very high mountain and show Him the nations of the world and all their glory. He dangled the world in front of Jesus, saying he would give it to Jesus if He would only kneel and worship him. All Jesus had to do was agree to take on being an earthly king over the world, forsake His heavenly Father, and be under Satan's rule ... and the world was all His. What a lie! Jesus was already the king! Jesus already owned the world. Satan knew it too, but he wanted Him to be king of *his* dark world.

It was at this point that Jesus tells Satan to go away. He quotes from the scriptures, "Jesus said to him, 'Away from me, Satan! For it is written: Worship the Lord your God, and serve him only'" (Matthew 4:10 NIV).

This third temptation was about pulling Jesus over to his side. He wanted Jesus's soul. He wanted to defeat the Lord of glory. He comes at us too, wanting our very own souls. He used the fact that Jesus is human as the rest of us are. He tried to talk Jesus into using his power for his own earthly gain (his human side), especially since Satan is the power of this world. Jesus was in the position of being able to make anything happen that He wanted to. Satan used this fact against Him in great temptation of giving in to the weakness of the flesh.

In every temptation, he was trying to get Jesus to put His earthly human side first. He was trying to get Him to put his flesh ahead of His divine spirit. He was trying to get Him to live for the world instead of for God. This is what he does to us too. Satan comes at us using materialism and power as the magnificent reasons to live and blinds us to the importance of the spirits of our very own souls and our eternal lives. Satan knows more about our egos than we do. He is sly and deceitful as he strokes our egos, telling us we can do this or that, and it will be okay … God will take care of us. Oh, what traps he sets; what webs he weaves! If dangling materialism and stroking the ego doesn't work, then there are always those words "power" and "control" that he slyly sneaks in.

He is real, he is evil, and he works hard. However, we have the Word that has the power to run him off. We have the gift of God's Holy Spirit inside of us that is greater than he is. Jesus passed the tests of temptations. Jesus is the perfect Lamb of God. He did not sin. We are not perfect yet. We have weaknesses, and we give in to sin. We have Jesus, who saves us when we fall into Satan's traps and schemes. He will help us get out of it when we are sorry and ask Him to help us. Jesus knows how hard it is. The spiritual warfare that was going on when Satan attacked Jesus was in full force. He came at a time when Jesus was in a weakened state. However, the temptation was halted by the Word of God that Jesus used. He was teaching us right then and there how to deal with temptation. It was a very hard battle for Jesus. We can't even begin to understand how hard it was for Him. It was serious and soul threatening, but when Jesus won the battle … listen to this … God sent angels to him. He didn't just send one angel to his Son, He sent *angels*. The angels took care of him. It was that bad of an ordeal. Now that is bad!

"Then the devil left him, and angels came and attended him" (Matthew 4:11 NIV).

I know that angels were surrounding me the day that Satan told me he had my son. I could not have withstood Satan's direct attack without the power of God protecting me. I am deeply thankful to my Father for taking care of me.

We are not safe from Satan in this world. He will always come after us. We won't be safe until we are in the arms of God. However, God helps us while we are here. The Lord in me defeated Satan that day on top of that mountain in Tennessee. Faith in my God, my Savior, and the Holy Spirit, the great Three in One, helped me to stand up to him and send him away. I told him the truth, and he went away. Jesus told him the truth, and he went away. Satan just hates the truth. The truth is more powerful than he is. It is the truth that sets us free from him. We must live in the truth for victory. Satan knows that nothing can separate us from the love that God has for us that is through His Son, Jesus Christ our Lord. Satan hates it, but he knows it. This truth is our weapon.

> For I am convinced that neither death nor life,
> neither angels nor demons,
> neither the present nor the future,
> nor any powers,
> neither height nor depth,
> nor anything else in all creation,
> will be able to separate us from the love of God
> that is in Christ Jesus our Lord.
> —Romans 8:38 (NIV)

DEAR JEREMY

It is two days before your birthday as I write this. On July 11, 1978, you came into this world, and now I must face the day of your birth without you. For the first time, I had an impression of letting you go. I woke up at 7:30 a.m. with this impression on me. I really did. I cannot distinctly remember details, but it was there. Was it from you, Jeremy? Are you helping in this letting-go process? It has only been two months since you left. Did I actually let go of something? If I did, what was it? I felt a release or an urge to release. I felt a rising to the sky coming from my body. It felt like paper floating upward in the wind.

Then the pain set in, the unbearable pain of facing your first birthday on earth without you here. Then sweet memories came in with a painful rush. You were such a good baby, so quiet and sweet. You didn't fuss much; you were so busy entertaining yourself with your surroundings. I wish I had you back. I am in a state of alternating back and forth. I want you back, I miss you, and at the same time I am trying to let you go.

I am so glad that you followed your heart in being yourself. You succeeded because your death has had a huge impact on this county. Only an honest, genuine, and loving person could have done this.

How many times did you tell me how much your friends loved your car? Remember what I always told you? I always told you that it wasn't the car; it was the boy driving the car! Remember that?

I am thankful you were true to your values, honest and humble. I know that God was not taken by surprise when you showed up. He is the one who numbers our days and knows why. You had a purpose; it was fulfilled, but you will live on in people's hearts. You touched many people in so many ways that will never be forgotten. I know this because they have told me.

There are some people who want to tell me that sin and the wrong choices took your lives. Well, I agree, yet I know this is only a part of the whole picture. I doubt that you were the only drinking, driving teen that night. You just happen to be one that didn't come home.

We all fall short of the glory of God. We are all sinners, and some live to tell about it, some get by with it, and some keep doing it. Some get past it to become great witnesses for our Lord in telling their stories while encouraging and helping others. The different outcomes of sinful behaviors are numerous. Results happen in different ways to all of us and to those around us due to our sinfulness, but it is what God does with those results that can make good come from bad.

We know and you know what impact choices can have on our lives; however, life and death are not totally in our hands. God did not do this tragic thing, but He allowed it to happen according to His plan and His purpose and His all-encompassing wisdom and love.

You know, Jeremy, how I tried to commit myself and my family to the Lord in all things. I know I have failed over and over due to my humanness, my weaknesses, and my bad choices, but my intentions have always been the same. I know that God can take bad and make good come out of it. I have seen it happen too many times. He is love, and He is light. I know you are with Him, and I will not believe anything else. If I believed otherwise, my life would not be worth living, and everything that I have lived for would all be in vain. Everything that I fought for, prayed for, lived for would mean nothing to me, and I would lay down my life and die. But I choose life. I choose to trust God and His everlasting love and mercy. I choose to realize that I don't have all the answers, and I won't until I reach heaven's glory.

I am not denying that you made wrong choices; you know yourself that you did. What I am saying is that we humans do not have all the answers, but God does. We cannot neatly arrange this all out on the table and put it in order as to why and how. We can look at facts, we can look at cause and effect, but how could we even think that in our human form we know all the answers? Of course, we know for a fact that drinking and driving do not mix ... they are deadly, and they are wrong. We never know who will be spared from its destruction and who won't. You didn't understand how fragile and precious life is. You didn't understand how one choice could mean the difference between life and death.

All of us are unique, made by the hand of God, and only God knows everything about us. I would have been a wiser mother if I had made it a daily habit of asking God what you needed each and every day. I didn't do that, and I have repented to you and to the Lord. I know you forgive me and God forgives me. I cannot go back and change a thing; I know I can only go forward.

Of course, we can speculate and see for ourselves the consequences of our sins, but this is not to say that we see the whole picture, which is in God's sight only. He is the one who forms this network of life on earth. Who is to blame for this tragedy? This has been a major concern to many. When it comes right down to it, we all are guilty. We are all in this together, and there is no way out of it. We are one. If I were to blame myself entirely, you entirely, the field party entirely, the person who sold or gave you the drinks entirely, your speed entirely, others entirely, I would go crazy, stark-raving mad.

I know that God does not look the other way when any of His children die. He *knows*. The Bible says He even knows every time a sparrow falls. I have to give it all to God and trust Him completely in this madness and know beyond a shadow of a doubt that He knows best when a person should live and when he or she has completed their life's work. I know that the hand of God could have intervened, and it would have changed the entire picture. But it didn't happen. I give it all to God. I trust in His tender, loving care. You were given to me for a little while, and for that I am thankful. Now, you have gone back to the One who gave you life.

I wonder why I see the world so differently now. Has your death given me more insight into what is real and true? Before this, I thought everything centered around this earth. I am not talking about the sun, moon, or planets and how the universe works. I am talking about spiritual things that we cannot see and know nothing about. That was really selfish of me, wasn't it? Now, I see that everything centers around God, and I should revolve around God, who knows how all things work. It is time for me to give everything to His all-knowing care and let go of thinking I have control and I have all answers. It is time for me to accept.

Oh, how I wish I had tapped into your great mind! As a parent, I was so busy trying to take care of your physical needs and teaching you right from wrong that I didn't take time to probe into your spirit and truly get to know you. What joy I missed, but I know that I will be given a second chance when I see you again. I believe this with all my heart.

I have felt your great love for me since you died. You have wrapped your arms around me in your spirit, and I have felt a love that is greater and more complete than is possible in this life on earth. You have helped me tremendously through your death by staying close by in your spirit. If you feel the desire to travel on, then you must go. I do not want you to stay here and be burdened by this old world's troubles and pain. As your cousin Davy wrote to me, "Soon enough we will be with you." I thought that was very wise for a teenager to express. He understands that life is short no matter how long we live. Life is short compared to eternity. I know that the time will pass faster for you because there is no time in eternity.

Your death has shown me the wisdom, love, friendship, and power that teenagers possess. Even in their struggle within themselves to become adults, they have an underlying power that is wondrous. I know that teenagers are in a dramatic stage of life, experiencing an abundance of everything and all things on this earth. Their perception is keen and startling even though they may not realize it fully or be aware of its potential. Everything they experience is monumental to their growth toward adulthood. I remember my own teen years, when "being" was what mattered. I sucked in every experience, not totally aware of what was happening but holding on to it steadfastly. It seems that of all the years, the teen years are the most experimental with curiosity and keen perception of being, of wanting to know, of wanting to feel, and of wanting to experience life. Bit by bit, teens receive freedom of moving toward adulthood and utilizing it in many ways according to their personalities, values, knowledge, and past experiences. Sometimes, understanding is not forthright in coming, especially in their mortality. I know that I lacked understanding and knowledge as I grew up. Everyone does. The thing is that even now I still lack these things, and

I realize this will always be. No matter how much I still tend to grow in knowledge and wisdom, there will always be more.

You had a hard-knuckle determination to be yourself, as you told us many times. Even though you were shy, you were determined. I think your shyness was basically the fact that you were embarrassed easily. You did not want attention directed in your way. You wanted to blend and be a part of the whole but not lose yourself in the process. And now the attention of the entire county is focused on you. This is the way it is right now, and I know that you wouldn't like it. However, I know that you are different now, and you see things as they really are; you see the whole picture, not just the bits and pieces that I see.

After writing all of this, I know that this letting-go feeling is a process that I will probably feel at different times and at different stages of my grief. Talking to you about all of this has helped me release thoughts, feelings, and speculations and has given me the realization that even though you will not physically be here with us for your birthday, you are still with us in a more profound way than ever before. I love you with all my heart and soul, and I look forward to the day when I will see you again.

Love,
Mom

Are not two sparrows sold for a penny?
Yet not one of them will fall to the ground
apart from the will of our Father.
And even the very hairs of your head are all numbered.
So don't be afraid; you are worth more than many sparrows.
—Matthew 10:29–31 (NIV)

LIKE A ROCK

It had been about three months, I think, when I felt the urge to talk to the teenagers of our hometown. They were hurting from the tragedy, and they were searching for answers. My heart was tugged to speak to them. I knew who was doing the tugging of my heart. It was obvious to me that God wanted me to do this because I knew I could not do this on my own.

I called Leland and told him that I wanted to speak to his youth group, which included youth from the seventh through the twelfth grades and from several other churches. These were wonderful kids, and I looked forward to being with them. We set a date, and I went prepared to pour out my feelings about Jeremy, the tragedy, the experiences I was having, and most of all I wanted to convey to them how much God loves them.

I started out playing a song on the tape player. I chose "Like a Rock" by Bob Seger. When the tape finished, I explained why I chose that song and what it had to do with what I had to say.

I told them that we liked that song so much because it reminded us of Jeremy. He was like a rock, big and strong. He had big, strong arms and legs. I used to tease him about his muscles, saying, "Let me see those muscles." I would feel them and say, "Well, what happened to them?" (Of course, they would feel like big, hard rocks, but I would insist they were just plain puny.) He would grin and go pump some more weights. He loved it; he knew I was teasing him.

Road Trip: Jesus, Jeremy and Me

His eyes were clear, and his hands were steady, just like all the eyes and hands of those teenagers I was talking to. They were young! I explained that my hands weren't quite as steady as they once were; nor was my eyesight as good as it used to be. It happens in life just like Bob Seger's song says it does. These things happen as we age. But I had Jeremy, who read small print for me on medicine bottles and who threaded those little bitty holes in needles for me. Jeremy helped me a lot; however, he left while he was still young and strong. He was not going to get to age.

I emphasized how he thought nothing would ever happen to him. He would always say, "Don't worry about me. I'll be okay." He never gave consideration that anything would or could ever happen to him, so he never thought about how it would affect us or others. I know that is what we think when we are young and healthy, and I wanted to get the message across to them that things can and do happen. I knew they knew this. They were experiencing the loss of their friends, yet I wanted them to apply it to themselves.

I talked about the value of friendships. I told them I didn't think Jeremy had a clue about how many friends he had. I knew that we didn't have a clue. He was very shy. He talked to me about it because he didn't like the fact that he was shy. This didn't seem to make any difference because he still was able to form strong friendships all over the county with both girls and boys. When we went to the high school to gather his belongings, we talked to the principal about Jeremy. He said it was unbelievable how this had affected so many teens at the school. He said that usually when a teen dies, it affects the groups that he or she was associated with the most. However, he said that Jeremy had crossed all lines with all groups and affected the entire school.

"How did he do it?" I asked.

The answer that I received from so many was this: "He took them one at a time and made genuine friendships with each one."

But he didn't know. He didn't have a clue how many loved and cherished his friendship.

I wanted these teens to realize the preciousness of their lives and how much they were loved by their families, their friends, and their communities. These were some of the things that I spoke about to the group at church. I wanted to express to them how special they were, even if they didn't feel special. I knew there were probably some there who were shy as Jeremy was, yet he was loved by many, and so were they. I told them that Jeremy's life was a miracle, given by God and now with God.

I told them they were God's greatest miracle, above every other creature on this great earth.

"You are fashioned in the image of God Almighty Himself," I said. "You are made in His likeness, and He breathed your spirit into you in your mother's womb. The angels rejoice over you when you accept Jesus Christ as your Lord and Savior. If you make the angels happy, then just think how happy God must be!"

It was my purpose to let them know Jeremy knew how much they loved and missed him and how much his absence grieved their hearts. I was there to comfort them, uphold them, and give love to them. The most important message I had to give them was about God's unconditional love toward them. I wanted to emphasize the value of their youth, their uniqueness, and their lives on this earth.

I know that Satan works hard on our children, on our youth. He bombards them, and one of his powers lies in undermining their self-images blinding them to who they really are. He should not get away with this. It makes me burn with anger. He lies profusely, and he steals precious lives. This should be a well-known fact, but it doesn't seem to be. How else can we fight it unless we know the facts? This is the way it is, and everyone should be aware of his schemes, no matter what age they are. This doesn't just affect teenagers.

I urged them to love themselves, take care of themselves, and believe in themselves.

I left as soon as I was finished. I was not strong enough to talk personally to any of them. I knew that I had done what I came to do. I loved them. I wanted them to know how much God loved them.

Part VI

PRESENCE ON EARTH AND IN HEAVEN

PRESENCE

I know more about what our presence means.

I learned it when Jeremy's presence was gone. His presence was gone from us in an instant, and then he was present with the Lord. This change of presence left a void on earth that couldn't be filled with or by any other person or in any other way.

Presence is felt as much as it is seen or heard. It is felt in a room, at the kitchen table, in the car, at school, at church … presence is everywhere a spirit is. And when a presence is gone, it is felt as a harsh reality.

I remember at the funeral home that it did not matter what anyone had to say to me. People were worried about what to say, but that didn't matter. At that time, words meant nothing to me because my mind couldn't absorb them. In fact, I don't remember any words spoken to me at the funeral home. My son was lying in a casket, and there wasn't one word that could make me feel better. I felt dead inside. What I do remember is people just being there, and that was all I needed. People were everywhere, inside and outside, and I was comforted just knowing they were there. Their presence was what mattered. Words could not take away my pain, but their presence was a comfort. Their presence helped to hold me up. Their eyes spoke volumes, and their hugs were living things, and handshakes had great healing power.

Talking about our presence here, I have asked myself at times, "Now, just why am I here on this earth?"

Have you ever wondered that? And then God spoke to my heart, telling me I am here because He put me here! That's pretty simple, isn't it?

He put us here, and we are here to do His will. This is His plan. He made us like this on purpose. He made us different from any other living creature. He made us in His own image and in His likeness. We are like our Father! Oh, that is so exciting! He blessed us and said to be fruitful and multiply, filling the earth with ourselves. He wants us here!

That doesn't mean that everybody has to get married or that everybody has to have children. No, it doesn't mean that at all. There are plenty of people here to do that job. We are all different. He said to take care of the birds, the fish, every other living creature and the earth itself. Does everybody take care of a bird? No. Does everybody take care of fish? No. We all have different jobs to do. Each job, though different, is important. He gave us work to do, whatever that might be. We are not to sit around doing nothing. As His children, He wants us to work, learn from life, learn about faith, learn from each other, help others, let others help us as needed, lean on Him for support, love Him, love ourselves in a healthy way, love others as we love ourselves, obey Him, have fellowship with Him, worship Him, and tell others about His Son.

This whole earth and all of the people in it are important to Him. Each and every job we do matters to God. Our presence here on this earth is a grand thing! We show how much we love Him when we love others. That's what He wants!

When Jesus came, He gave more information and instructions. He told us more about our future, about life after physical death. Our presence in heaven is going to be totally different than it is here on earth. For one thing, there will be no marriage.

The Saducees had a question for Jesus about marriage in heaven. The question in itself was interesting because they didn't even believe in resurrection. They thought they were being smart and tricky, but Jesus knew their hearts. Well, anyway, here was their question: if a woman's husband died and she married six other times and they all had died, then whose wife would she be in heaven?

"Jesus replied, 'You are in error because you do not know the Scriptures or the power of God. At the resurrection people will neither marry nor be given in marriage; they will be like the angels in heaven'" (Matthew 22:29–30 NIV).

There is their answer about the marriage. But Jesus knew they didn't even believe in the resurrection, so He went a step further in His answer. "But about the resurrection of the dead—have you not read what God said to you? 'I am the God of Abraham, the God of Isaac, and the God of Jacob.' He is not the God of the dead but of the living. When the crowds heard this, they were astonished at his teaching" (Matthew 22:31–33 NIV).

Jesus says that God is the God of Abraham, the God of Isaac, and the God of Jacob. He is not the God of the dead but of the living! He *is* their God, not *was* their God. They are not dead; they are alive! Don't you just love Jesus's answer? To be absent from the body is to be present with the Lord if we belong to Him. This is what happened to one of the thieves who hung on the cross right there beside Jesus.

> One of the criminals who hung there hurled insults at him: "Aren't you the Christ? Save yourself and us!" But the other criminal rebuked him. "Don't you fear God," He said, "since you are under the same sentence? We are punished justly, for we are getting what our deeds deserve. But this man has done nothing wrong." Then he said, "Jesus, remember me when you come into your kingdom." Jesus answered him, "I tell you the truth, today you will be with me in paradise." (Luke 23:39–43 NIV)

This criminal believed that Jesus was who He said He was. He asked Jesus to remember him when he came into His kingly glory. Jesus said the most beautiful thing to him. He told him that it would be as soon as that very day! On that very day that he died, he would be with Jesus in paradise! As soon as his spirit came out of his body, he would be with Jesus. Oh my, my, my! What a beautiful answer.

How do we explain that? That thief did not have time to be baptized, did he? He was hanging on a cross. His life here on earth was almost over. This thief was in a position where it was impossible to be baptized. Jesus knew this man's heart had changed and that he believed in Him. He knew he was sincere, and Jesus knew this thief could not be baptized. As I've said before, Jesus deals with each person on an individual basis. Jesus accepted his repentance and his confession of faith right there at death's door.

Paul wrestled with wanting to die and go on to heaven. Ever felt that way before? He went back and forth on it. Paul was tired. He had been through so much that he knew it would be wonderful for him to be there with the Lord. He also knew his presence was needed here on earth until his work was done. He knew his time wasn't up. Paul says this:

> For to me, to live is Christ and to die is gain. If I am to go on living in the body, this will mean fruitful labor for me. Yet what shall I choose? I do not know! I am torn between the two: I desire to depart and be with Christ, which is better by far, but it is more necessary for you that I remain in the body. Convinced of this, I know that I will remain, and I will continue with all of you for your progress and joy in the faith, so that through my being with you again your joy in Christ Jesus will overflow on account of me. (Philippians 1:21–26 NIV)

Paul had met the Lord that day on the road to Damascus, and it had changed his life forever. Paul couldn't wait to get to heaven to be with the Lord. But he loved people and knew they needed him. He knew he could continue to help them. He wanted to show them how their joy in Jesus could overflow! (Overflowing joy!) Doesn't that sound wonderful?

Paul was a good man after he met the Lord. He was a hardworking man, an interesting man, such a Christian. He lived through so many trials here on earth, but he never gave up. Satan worked big-time, overtime in trying to defeat Paul because Paul was accomplishing so much for the Lord Jesus. But Paul kept on fighting the good fight and keeping the faith. Through all of this, Paul needed others' support too. He needed people. He needed encouragement. He gave thanks to God when others refreshed his spirit, when others brought him food and clothing, and when others stood by him supporting him in any way that he needed. Paul's presence on this earth was important. All those present who supported his ministry were important.

Besides taking care of the earth, taking care of everything in it, and taking care of each other in it, Jesus tells us our whole work on earth is wrapped up into two commandments. Love God first and then love others as much as we love ourselves. These commandments were what Paul worked so very hard to do. He started churches for the Lord Jesus Christ no matter how difficult it was or how impossible it seemed. Nothing stopped him! And then he kept in contact with these churches to help them. He didn't abandon them. He didn't forget about them. He taught, strengthened, comforted, encouraged, and prayed for them. He knew this was his job to do here on this earth. He was true to himself. He loved himself when he was true to God first, true to himself second, and true to others.

This is what we are supposed to do for each other. We are here for each other to complete the Master's plan. Paul's presence in this world was powerful.

Our presence in this world is powerful too!

God created the world for a very important reason, or He would not have done it in the first place. (That makes sense to me.) We are important, and our lives mean something. This is the way He wants it for now, until the world ends. Jesus said that whenever I do something for someone else, I am doing it for Him. What a powerful thought! Even if I am sitting down listening to someone who needs to talk, I am doing it for the Lord. Even if I am exercising and planning a healthy menu, I am doing it for the Lord. I am to love myself in a healthy way as well as love others. We serve the Living God by serving each other and being there for each other. To be present with someone is what is important but only if we add something to it. That something is love and showing that love by helping in any way that is needed. Helping others is not for our own gain so we can get something out of it or get paid back. Helping others is helping the Lord. Living is in giving, whether it is laughing with someone, sitting with someone, crying with someone, listening to someone, talking to someone, taking food to someone, or telling others about Jesus. The list goes on and on and on.

Presence is important on earth and in heaven. No matter where we are, here or at home with the Lord, our presence matters to God.

When Jeremy died, people sat with me. They surrounded my bed when I couldn't get up. When Jeremy was in the funeral home, I remember my grandmother Moma Eva sitting beside me. She is my daddy's mother. I could not say one word to her. She did not say one word to me, but I knew she was there. She had been through this same pain when her son Bobby died. We knew each other's pain, and so we sat together without a word, just being present for each other. Moma Eva is gone now as I write this, but she was very important in my life. I have good memories of her and her house. I remember sleeping upstairs with my cousins and smelling ham cooking for breakfast. I remember how she wore bonnets when she was out in the sun. She killed and dressed chickens and then made the best chicken and dumplings. She loved going to Sunday school and church every Sunday and enjoyed church revivals every summer. She learned to play the piano and organ in her later years when I was a little girl. She wanted to teach me, but I wasn't interested, but oh, how she loved to play those instruments! She cooked for work hands during tobacco-working seasons and loved talking on the phone. I remember being at her house and that old pressure cooker would be singing, and the phone would be ringing, and life was wonderful! Moma Eva was a source of strength to me by just sitting next to me at that funeral home. Her presence was powerful.

People touched my shoulder, hugged me, kissed me, and acknowledged my pain. That was such a comfort! They sent cards, notes, and letters that we read over and over and over when we felt like it. Their presence was in those words. They left messages on the answering machine, and we listened to those messages over and over when we were home and needed someone else's presence with us. They brought food. Within each act of kindness was healing balm. Their presence was there in each and every thing they did. They have never to this day abandoned us.

Being there for someone is quite powerful. Paul says it refreshed his spirit when his friends came to visit. We need each other. Sending presence in any form is powerful. The acts of presence, which are being there, listening, loving, sharing, and giving of ourselves, are powerful acts of love. There is such power in our very presence no matter what form when given in love.

Jeremy's presence is missed and always will be. It has been twenty years now since his death. All of us still miss him very much. It is comforting to know that now he is in the presence of the Lord. And even though I cannot physically see Him, I know that God is always present with me. And I can honestly say I would not have wanted to miss this earthly life. Of course there are times of horrible pain, but there are also times of happiness and joy. We build these times and these moments together with our presence with each other.

Our presence is now here on this earth, but one day our presence will be with the Lord. We will also be present with our loved ones and everyone else who has gone before us. We have so much to look forward to! Our presence matters no matter where we are. Our presence never ends. Our presence is beautiful.

God is so good. God is ever present. Praise His holy name!

CHURCH

I found out church was one of the hardest places to go. Oh, yes, it was.

Who would have thought it? I didn't understand it. You see, ever since I was a child, I have loved going to church. It has always been a deep passion of mine. I loved God so (still do), and Sunday was actually my favorite day of the week. It became very painful to go there after Jeremy died. This really surprised me. It just didn't make any sense to me either. Why would church be the hardest place to go?

When I was getting dressed, a stab of pain would run though me that I would not be going into his room anymore to wake him up. This happened Sunday after Sunday for a long time.

The first time I went after he died, I had to leave and go outside ... right during the very first song. I cried my heart out. I missed Jeremy being there sitting right beside me. This happened the next Sunday, and then the next one, and then almost every Sunday morning that I went. This went on for many months. It might not be during the first song, but it would be sometimes during the service. When I would go out to my car and cry on these Sunday mornings, I gave thanks after my tears stopped flowing. I was so thankful that he had sat beside me. His dad played the organ, so it was Jeremy and I who sat together. Julie was already married and went to another church with Brian and Dustin. After my crying and my thanking

God, then I would go back in and try to stay. Sometimes I would have to go outside more than once during the service.

Jeremy and I had a special relationship in church. He picked on me a lot, punching me a little, offering me chewing gum, or asking me if I had any. Sometimes, he playfully held on to the empty communion cup before taking mine or giving me his, and then he would put them in their slots. All these little things that I took for granted seemed to mean the most now that he was gone. He had one pair of jeans that I guess he designated as official church jeans. I close my eyes, and I see them over and over in my mind along with his big, black tennis shoes. The way he elbowed me, or told me I was singing too loud, or got after me when I didn't put any money in the collection plate are some of my sweetest memories that I cherish.

He was gone in an instant. Never again would I wake him so he could get ready. Never again would I hear that car of his rumble into the church parking lot, and never again would he sit beside me. That part of my life was over. Tears and pain had taken its place.

I didn't give up. I kept going back, and I kept going out to the car to cry and then going back in again. It took several months before I could sit through a full service without leaving. It took longer than that before I could sing again. I had no song in me.

Why is church so hard? I pondered it, and I asked the Lord to help me understand.

The answers came, and they were profound. I sat in amazement from this newfound knowledge. I sat in awe of the miracle of church. And that is what it is. It is truly a miracle.

Church is the one place where the believers of God come together in unison and agreement to worship God. That is why we are there. We are God-centered. He is the reason for our presence. We may not all agree on all the decisions that are made in keeping a church going, but we are all there because we believe in God and have come to worship Him. This does not have to be in an official church building. It can be anywhere that believers meet together to worship God.

We all become one in a sweet savor of agreeing that Jesus Christ is the Son of God. Together, we are joined with Him as we sing praises to His name. We sing together, we listen together, and we sit together in love and adoration of our Creator. This togetherness is being united as one in love and harmony. We are the bride of Christ.

It takes discipline and strength to continue going to church because our enemy Satan hates it. He will use anything and everything to keep us out of its doors. God knows what we have to overcome. He knows we are putting Him first when we get there. He delights in our coming!

The Holy Spirit is in each of us, and when we come together, we are multiplied in love! This great love is permeated throughout the whole room! It is God-filled! Love abounds everywhere and binds us together, making us strong and purposeful. This is what church is about. Church is about love, love for the Father, love for the Son, love for the Holy Spirit, love for ourselves, and love for others.

It is not about committees, board meetings, church programs, or any of the stuff we organize to do. They are not the purpose; they are the helpers in the purpose. It is imperative to keep in mind who we are working for in all of those places that contribute to the work of the church, and it is crucial that we let Him lead and not take it over ourselves. It is of great importance to remember that Satan sends his demons to church to help him in his work, which is to destroy our congregations in any way he can. He searches for our weaknesses and starts to work on them. He wants us to look bad to the world, so he works in any little weakness he can find. Of course, the weaknesses are there because we are human. We have to be alert and on guard. He had the nerve to interfere in the Garden of Eden, didn't he? He has no problem trying to interfere in our churches. His work is to tear down what we build up. His work is to make conflict, cause confusion, insert jealously, lure away, destroy; the list is endless.

When we study God's Word together, we become united and strong. Love is to be our greatest aim. Loving God, Jesus, and the Holy Spirit first is paramount to a healthy church.

Let me tell you what happened to me. I was sitting in church one Sunday morning, and God allowed me to see something that was very reverent and holy. I saw with my spirit eyes love vapors rising out of every head that was present! It was a wow-oh-wow moment! Yes, I could see these vapors, and they all looked alike! The love-vapors went straight up toward heaven, and God was receiving them with great love toward us! It was an absolutely beautiful sight! I knew He was receiving them, and He loved each and every one of them. I was awestruck at this powerful vision.

It was (and is) the power of the Holy Spirit in each of us sending up these love vapors from inside us because we love the Lord Jesus Christ! It is the uniting of the church (we are the bride of Christ) with Jesus (who is the husband.) It is the power of love from Jesus, who bought us with a great price (with His life and His blood), that is in church during worship that makes it miraculous!

All of this coming together with all of this unseen power is a love offering to the Lord. Since I have seen this vision of how God receives our love vapors being poured out to Him in church, it is my hope and prayer that I never take church for granted. Church is a miracle bought and paid for by the precious blood of the Lord Jesus Christ. We belong to Him.

The believers who have passed on are watching us from heaven. Hebrews 12:1 tells us that the people of God who have died are surrounding us in a great cloud. I have mentioned this before, and I love it. They are our witnesses, our cheerleaders, and with this in mind, we should give up anything that hinders us or holds us back from running this Christian race here on earth. The many people of great faith from the Old Testament (all the way back to the beginning of time) are in this group. They are championing us to keep going ... keep going. They love us as their brothers and sisters in Christ. They were not perfect in their lives down here. They know how hard it is. But they did not give up. Church is earthly and heavenly united by all Christians, some here and some gone on. It is united by God's great Holy Spirit. When we walk out of the door of church to face another week, we have lots of support from heaven with us if we recognize, acknowledge, and use it. We are never alone in our work as Christians. We are the church even when we walk out of church. It is who we are. What power and support we have all around us. Glory hallelujah!

The Lord loves His church. He died for the church. He started the church before He died. His disciples were His first members. He spent time with them in the Judean countryside, and His disciples baptized people (John 3:22). He instituted the Lord's Supper, teaching them about His broken body and the blood He was going to shed. He told them to take the bread and eat it and take the cup and drink from it. He said it would be the last time He would eat and drink it with them, but He would drink it again with them in heaven. Isn't that exciting to think we will eat and drink with Jesus in heaven? Jesus brought in singing too. Then they sung a hymn together after they ate (Matthew 26:17–30)! Luke tells us that He said to keep doing the Lord's Supper in remembrance of Him (Luke 22:14–20). Jesus told them how to deal with sin in the church (Matthew 18:15–17). Jesus taught his disciples how to pray. Jesus instituted preaching, teaching, baptizing, the Lord's Supper, prayer, singing, and how to get along in His church. He taught by example. These are the things we still do today.

After Jesus ascended into heaven, there were 126 members of His church waiting just like Jesus told them to. The bride (church) was going to receive the power of the great Holy Spirit. Acts 2:2 tells us how it happened. Seven weeks after Jesus's death and resurrection, the Holy Spirit came to the house where the believers were meeting. Yes, the Holy Spirit came to the house! The Holy Spirit was going to do something very special. It happened on one of the Jewish holidays called the day of Pentecost.

The believers meeting in this house heard the roaring of a great, mighty wind above the house, and then it started blowing through the house. Then, here came fire!

It looked like flames or tongues of fire on each person's head, and each one present was filled with the Holy Spirit and started speaking in different languages.

There was a reason for this! God had chosen this day to send the Holy Spirit in a mighty way. Since the day of Pentecost was a very big celebration, there were many Jews in Jerusalem from many different nations. They spoke different languages, and this is how God's Holy Spirit was going to teach thousands of Jews in one day. Three thousand were baptized. Can you imagine such a thing? They joined the other believers in regular attendance at the apostles' teaching sessions and for communion services and prayer meetings. The church was on fire! The first church was started with great power of wind and passion of fire! The church grew and grew, and then the persecution of the church started. The believers spread out across the country. It was at the church of Antioch that the believers were first called Christians (Acts 11:26).

We are Christians all over the world now. We are the church of Jesus Christ.

We are His bride, and He is our groom.

We are not to neglect His church! We are His bride.

"Let us not give up meeting together, as some are in the habit of doing, but let us encourage one another—and all the more as you see the Day approaching" (Hebrews 10:25). This power and passion of the Holy Spirit is still with us. It is in us! The Holy Spirit will lead us in all truth and tell us what to do. We just have to tap into it and let Him lead!

God answered my prayer. It was the *power* of the church service that made it so hard for me to go when Jeremy was no longer with me.

I felt the loss of Jeremy's presence in church deeply. It is here that love abounds in abundance. It is here that love is multiplied by our coming together, and I was not even aware of it until Jeremy died!

The answers God gave to me about church have given me untold strength in my faith of going to church. These answers have given me even greater love for each one present and lots of respect for each one present whether I agree with everything or not! They have taught me about the great beauty and meaning of our coming together to worship God, how it makes us stronger in our faith and especially what it means to Him. It is not just about the fact that we are supposed to go to church. It is about the love of being the bride of Christ and meeting Him as our husband, worshipping Him, praying together to Him, singing together to Him, communing together with Him during His Lord's Supper. This is what is important to God! It is about faithfulness to God the Father, Jesus the Son, and the Holy Spirit.

The pain I felt in church was from all of these things that I could not see with my physical eyes. It was the pain of our separation from this wonderful, beautiful, spiritual place called church. I couldn't see it, but I could feel it immensely. Jeremy's physical absence had also taken his spiritual presence away from sitting beside me! It had also taken away his love vapors going up into heaven! They had been a powerful influence on me while he was sitting beside me, even though at the time I didn't know it.

It was a painful letting-go process.

I look back at this now as a beautiful pain to carry with me always and to remember. It is one of those precious memories that we sing about. These are more jewels to store in heaven.

Now, I look at each individual in church and recognize his or her preciousness to our loving God.

Jeremy's last words to us were, "I'll see you at church in the morning." This was no accident that he said those words. He told us the truth. We will see him again, and we will all gather together at that one great church service in the heavens because we are the bride. The church is the reason Jesus came to earth to die! We are His. These love vapors are multiplied all over the world on Sunday morning (or any other time) as believers meet together to worship God. I feel more connected to churches everywhere now that I have had this experience. I visit many churches. These are God's people everywhere I go. I know we are all one. We are not to get sidetracked, focused on, or obsessed with denominationalism. As I sit in any church I am in, I visualize love vapors all over the world going up to God the Father and Jesus His Son. I feel united with other believers. There will be no divisions among us in heaven. All churches will be one. We are the bride of Christ. We will sing praises to God forever. We will take these beautiful memories of going to church with us. They will always be a part of us, a very beautiful part that God loves dearly.

> Let us hold unswervingly
> to the hope we profess,
> for He who promised
> is faithful.
> And let us consider
> how we may spur one another on toward love and good deeds.
> Let us not give up meeting together,
> as some are in the habit of doing,
> but let us encourage one another—and all the more
> as you see the Day approaching.
> —Hebrews 10:23–25 (NIV)

A FAMILY VISITOR

Julie called and asked if I would come out to her house and keep Dustin while she went to work. She needed a babysitter that day. Of course, I went.

I had no idea what this would stir up in me.

The whole day, I was confused. Was this baby Dustin or was he Jeremy? It was just like taking care of Jeremy when he was a baby. I fed Dustin and played with him. He was sleepy, so I rocked him and put him down for a nap. I sat on the couch to rest too, and it was then that I was consumed by memories of Jeremy as a baby. I cried while Dustin slept. I cried and I cried, and my whole body shook with grief.

I wanted my baby back.

"Father in heaven, I want him back," I wailed. The wanting and the longing were so intense that I was emotionally distraught. I missed Jeremy in such a deep and profound way that I even physically held out my arms for him. My arms ached for him.

I was a mess.

I cried out loud. I cried silently. I mourned and mourned while Dustin slept peacefully in his crib.

And then I stopped crying. I just knew someone was in the room with me! I felt a presence! Then I *smelled* someone I knew! The smell grew closer and closer.

It was my grandmother! I just knew it was my other grandmother. She is my mother's mother. I would know that smell anywhere. Nobody else in the world had her smell. This was Mom-maw Brown for sure!

She had died in January that year, 1996, and Jeremy had died in May. My Mom-maw Brown's spirit was in the room with me! I knew the instant that she sat down beside me and put her arms around me. I couldn't see her, but I felt her arms, and I could smell her. She held me and rocked me in her arms. Yes … she did!

I was surprised. No, I wasn't surprised; I was shocked! Yet I knew this was real. I could feel her, and I could smell her. I had not expected this to happen.

I didn't even know it *could* happen.

A sense of calm washed over me as I was rocked in her arms. She comforted me with her presence. She didn't have to say anything. Being with me was enough.

Mom-maw Brown was a hugger while she was on this earth. When we went to her house to see her, she met us at the door with arms flung open wide so we could melt right into her. And that's what we did.

When I think of her life here on earth, I think of the smell of her yeast rolls baking. She would have them in the oven about the time we were to arrive at her house for supper. Just thinking about those rolls made our mouths water. They were the best I have ever had. I think of her roses blooming outside in June as we hunted lightning bugs after dark while the adults sat in chairs watching us. The smell of roses wafted through the air as we ran in the fresh night air. I think of her rolling up her long gray hair and pinning it into a bun at the nape of her neck. I think of her taking her own mother, my great-grandmother Hahn, into her own home and taking care of her until she died. I think of her sewing clothes, making stuffed doll furniture, and her quilting. I think of the small motel that she and Granddaddy Brown owned and kept open to tourists until the Bluegrass Parkway was built. The new road took a lot of traffic away from Highway 62, where it was located, and they had to shut down the little motel. But before that happened, when we would visit them, we sat on the front porch talking to the tourists. That was an exciting time.

I think about when my granddaddy Brown fell off a ladder and broke his back and then Mom-maw Brown took care of him. They moved in room six so they could have peace and quiet while he healed. I think about when we (my family) moved in with them, staying in the house part of the motel to take care of it and keep it open. My daddy went back and forth to the farm during the day to do the work there. I remember that doorbell ringing at all hours of the night and my mother registering the tourists for a room. This was quite a change for Ricky, Karen, and me because now we lived in town and walked to elementary school. We rode the bus when we lived at home in the country. This was a big deal for little kids! When we got home from school, there was Mom-maw Brown waiting in room six with her arms wide open to welcome us back. We lived with them until Granddaddy Brown was well and they could take care of the motel again. Then we went back to our house at the farm.

I think of Mom-maw Brown's kindness and her gentleness. I think of her calm spirit, her happy smile, and her joy every time she saw us. I think about how she could make all her grandchildren feel like they were the favorite one! Mom-maw Brown loved the Lord with all her heart, and all her mind, and all her soul, and she loved her family and friends.

Peace, comfort, and love came from her spirit presence with me that day at Julie's house. I felt her concern for me, but more than that, I felt her love for me. I felt that she had seen and been with Jeremy. I felt her compassion, and I knew she knew I was having one of my unbearable moments. God had let her come to see me. Oh my! God is so good! She comforted me and stayed with me until I was calm and at peace.

What a miracle! I think now as I write this, why do I ever limit what God can do? Why do I ever put Him in a box of my own limitations? I am the one who is limited, not God. Everything about us is wondrous. Each of us has a distinctive smell, distinctive touch, and distinctive voice. In fact, every little thing about us is distinctive. I have more of an in-depth appreciation of this now.

Both of my grandmothers comforted me by their presence when Jeremy died. One was in physical form, and one was in spiritual form. Our Father in heaven had allowed this communication to be between us, between the spirit world and this physical world. He brought it all together by His great Holy Spirit. I didn't ask for it, but I received it and was so very grateful for it. It strengthened my spirit greatly.

God allowed Moses and Elijah to visit Jesus on a high mountain during His Transfiguration. Oh, how this must have strengthened Jesus.

What encouragement for him. What support for him for them to be there. He must have been so glad to see them.

Peter, James, and John were witnesses. When Peter saw them, he offered to build three shelters, one for Jesus, one for Moses, and one for Elijah. God immediately said no. He said, "This is my Son, whom I love; with him I am well pleased. Listen to Him!"

Moses and Elijah had been there. Even though they had been dead for years, they had been there with Jesus on that mountain. However, even though this really happened, God did not want Peter, James, and John to be confused about it and start worshipping the dead. We are never to worship the dead or become consumed with them. The dead are not to become our idols, our focal points, or our obsession.

I was to be grateful and in awe of God the Almighty, who allowed this great thing to happen to me. I am to keep my eyes on the Holy Trinity. Mom-maw Brown's visit was like the wind. I felt her, I experienced her, and I knew the effect she left on me and in me. She left peace and comfort. What a wonderful, powerful, loving visit! It came from the power of the Comforter, the great Holy Spirit.

MY VISIT FROM MARY

My grief went on for a long time. It would come and go. It was another day of grief in the summer of 1996. Again, I sat on the loveseat. This was my place, my space, my time with God early in the morning. As I talked to God, I cried, and I cried, and I cried. I couldn't help it. I still wanted Jeremy back. I had read that this feeling was normal. That helped a little bit, knowing I was normal.

This grief was raw and heavy. I simply wanted him back. I ached for him. It was very real, and the tears rolled and rolled. I just didn't think I could make it. What was I going to do?

"Dear God in heaven, how can I get through this?"

It was then that something monumental happened. Oh, yes, it did!

Mary came!

Mary came to visit me! Yes, she did!

Silently, she ushered herself into my living room.

Yes, I am talking about Mary, the mother of Jesus!

Oh my goodness, I couldn't believe it either! I knew it was her. I knew it. I knew it. I knew it! I did not have one doubt about it. It was a knowing that was within me, and it was there the very instant I sensed her presence with me.

Her presence filled the room, and yes, I stopped crying! Believe me, she had my full attention! I didn't hear her come in. I couldn't see her. I didn't smell one thing. I just knew her, and that was enough. Of course,

I wouldn't have recognized her by her smell or by her physical appearance anyway. I don't know what she looked like or smelled like. But I didn't need to know what she looked like or what she smelled like. Her presence said it all. Oh, man! Oh my goodness! I was stunned!

She sat down beside me. I sensed her presence there, and she was just as real as she would have been if she were physically, flesh and blood, sitting beside me. I could feel her presence, and it was powerful!

I did not expect this. In fact, this would have been the last thing in the world that I would have expected to happen. I didn't expect any of these things to happen to me that happened, and at that time, all I wanted was to have my Jeremy back!

She had sat down beside me, and with much compassion, she quietly said, "I know your pain. My son died too."

Doesn't that just choke you up? It choked me up to think about her pain, and it still does to this day. Oh, my dear, dear Mary!

She did not say this out loud. Her spirit spoke to my spirit.

"Oh, Mary," I cried. "How did you stand it?"

She didn't answer that. She didn't have to. I knew the answer in my heart. We don't have a choice about grief. It is as much a part of this world as anything else in it. God was with her in it. Her Son was with her in it, but that still didn't take away the physical pain and agony of being apart. It was through this visit that I came to understand that she had worked her way through her grief, just as I was working through mine. In fact, she had to work through it twice. I had never thought about that before.

It was bad enough, actually horrendous, to watch her son suffer and die, knowing all the time that He was as innocent, as sweet and as pure as a lamb. He was love, and she knew it, yet they had killed him. She did not really understand all of it or why it had to be that way. Jesus was dead, had been murdered for no reason, and that sword had struck her right in the heart and soul just as Simeon had predicted (Luke 2:33–35).

And then something wonderful beyond imagination had happened. Her Jesus, her baby, her precious Son came back to life again. She had wanted him back, and He had come back. She was so happy. But then, after Jesus came back to life on the third day, He didn't stay here on earth but a short while. She had Him for a few weeks. She was so happy to see Him, yet when He left to go to heaven, He was physically gone from her again. She missed her baby just as I was missing mine. His physical presence was gone from this earth. She felt the mother's grief deeply. That sword of death came back in the same spot, dangled there until her heart had shattered. Part of her physical body was gone too! Even though she knew He was (and is) the Messiah, even though she knew He was in heaven, she still grieved for Him, missing Him being with her, longing for Him, wanting Him back. She was His mother. He was a part of her.

She had gotten through it, and she knew I would get through it. We sat together in harmony, each knowing the grieving mother's pain. With her, she had brought peace and tranquility in the midst of my sorrow. It was the calm in the midst of the storm. It was the eye in the hurricane. It was the gentle center of the tornado.

I felt this genuine closeness to her as though I had always known her, and she had always known me. It's true! I felt that I had known her all my life. All my life! It was very real, and it was a feeling like no other feeling I had ever had. Even though I never knew Mary when she lived on this earth and she never knew me, I felt very close to her as if I had known her *all my life*. I know, I know, I am repeating myself, but it seems I can't help it! It was really amazing. It's not like Mary comes and visits every day! This was unbelievable, yet it was the reality of what was happening to me as I sat in my own living room.

I felt close to her heart, and she felt close to my heart as though we were the best of friends. Best friends with Mary, the mother of Jesus. What a feeling! Not only that, it felt as if we were family! Yes, family! And we are! We are adopted brothers and sisters of her Son, Jesus!

Oh, it was wonderful!

Her spirit spoke to my spirit, letting me know that she understood exactly the pain I was feeling. She had walked this walk when Jesus died. She knew from the beginning that her Son was the Son of God, but that did not take away her pain and agony of losing him physically from her on this earth. She had mourned for him from the depths of her soul, and she wanted her baby back just as I was doing.

Mary's presence was reassuring and ever so comforting. She soothed my broken heart with her presence. She calmed my frazzled nerves, and she stopped my tears for a time.

After she left, I sat in amazement! It was stunned amazement! I kept talking to her. I knew she would hear me. I apologized to her. I had never given Mary the honor that I should have. As the mother of our Lord Jesus, I thanked her, and I asked for her forgiveness in my lack of appreciating her complete love and obedience to God. I thanked her for what she went through. I recognized her pain, acknowledged it, and told her. I had always loved her in the Christmas story and had compassion for her at Easter time. I realized that was not enough. Now, she had my awe, respect, and honor as the mother of the human, physical part of my Lord and Savior Jesus Christ. I did not worship her. I worshipped her Son. That is what she wanted and wants for all people. She desires that all people hear about her Son, Jesus, believe in Him as their Savior, and worship Him as the Son of God. I agreed with her cousin Elizabeth who said to her in a loud voice, "Blessed are you among women, and blessed is this child you will bear" (Luke 1:42 NIV).

Of all the women in the entire world, she was the one Father God chose as the mother of His Son ... His only Son.

I greatly respected her, yet at the same time, she did not seem any different than me. She didn't want it any other way. She was humble and full of compassion. We were best friends and family.

I thanked God for the gift of the Holy Spirit, who makes these things possible. It was like the wind. I don't understand how it happened, where Mary came from or where she went to next, but now I know she stays very busy, and I know she loves all of us on earth who love her Son. We are all her best friends and her family.

I thought about heaven. Mary had proved to me that I will know everyone in heaven when I meet them there. It will not matter that I did not know them on earth. It will be a mutual, deep knowing of each and every person. There will be no strangers. We will all be best friends and family.

"Oh, God, you are so wonderful and majestic. How awesome are your powers! How long, how deep, how wide is your love for us your children. I praise your wonderful name. I fall on my knees in adoration and thankfulness. I serve the Living God, the Creator of the universe and everything in it. I belong to you and you only. Your faithfulness is beyond description. I have no words. I give you my mind, heart, and soul again. I give you my all. I know I will have to do this many times in my human life, and you know all about that. I thank you for always being there, always understanding, always willing to forgive. I thank you for sending Mary to comfort me. I thank you for our family, the family of God. I look forward to joining you and the rest of the family when my time comes. I love you," I prayed.

I looked at the Bible in my lap and turned to the book of Luke and decided I wanted to do a deep study about Mary with the Holy Spirit as my guide.

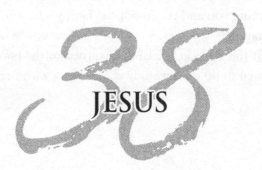

38
JESUS

The wedding feast was well under way when Mary heard they were out of wine. She went looking for her Son, so she could tell Him about it. He could fix this situation; she just knew He could. She had no doubt.

She found Him, but after she told Him the dilemma, He was reluctant to do anything. This did not stop Mary! No, it didn't. She insisted and even went so far as to tell the servants to do whatever He told them to do! What faith! What do you think about that? I know. It's mind-boggling.

He decided to give in to her request. I have always wondered about that. He had told His mother that His time had not come yet to do miracles, but He went ahead and performed His first one at this wedding! Mary knew who her Son was. Her faith was tremendous. She knew this was not a problem for her grown Son to do, and she did not give up! She had a mother's intuition that knew it would be okay. She had the faith that Jesus could do something about this! Her faith in Him and her persistence paid off. This must have been very important to her, don't you think? He realized how important this was to her. He loved His mother very much.

Jesus obliged His mother.

He spoke, and His words contained the power. He told the servants to fill six huge water pots with water, just plain water. After this was done, he told them to take some of it to the master of the wedding.

That's it? Just fill the pots with water and offer him a drink? Yes, that was all there was to it. Can you imagine how those servants felt when he told them to do that? They obeyed Him, though, no matter what they were feeling. They must have had a lot of respect for Mary and Jesus. The master took a drink and was so impressed with the taste of it that he gave the bridegroom a compliment, saying that the bridegroom had saved the best wine until now!

Wine? Did he say wine?

The master of the wedding did not know what had actually happened, and the servants were astonished that the water had turned to wine! Mary was pleased, the wedding master was impressed, and the bridegroom was complimented!

How did He do it?

He spoke with His mouth, telling the servants what to do, and it happened. It was a miracle, a supernatural event that only God can do (John 2:1–11).

That was the first miracle that Jesus did in public. It was the first of many miracles, so many that we do not have count of them. In fact, one of my favorite verses is John 21:25 (NIV).

"Jesus did many other things as well. If every one of them were written down, I suppose that even the whole world would not have room for the books that would be written."

Doesn't that just blow you away? When I ponder that verse, I just shake my head in wonderment. Thankfully, we have records of many of them in the four Gospels.

Word of mouth is really the best way to spread news, don't you think? It has power in it going from one person to another. It can spread quickly, and it sure did! We know that in today's world, it is easy to spread news with words on the phone, texting, Internet, and so on. Even without any of that, word got around in Jesus's day. It didn't take long before thousands of people followed Jesus after learning of His miracles.

Did you hear how Mary's Son, Jesus, fed five thousand men plus women and children with just five pieces of bread and two pieces of fish? Did you know that the disciples picked up twelve baskets full of pieces that were left over? How did He do it? What did He do? It's found in John 6:1–14.

He looked up to heaven to His Father. He gave thanks for the five pieces of bread and the two pieces of fish. He blessed them. He broke the loaves and the fish, handing pieces to His disciples to give out to the people. The bread and the fish just kept multiplying as He kept breaking them! That's it! There were over five thousand people who witnessed it! They were people who did not bring any food with them, and they were hungry. Evidently they didn't even think they would be staying long enough to eat food. They couldn't pull themselves away from Him. When the people realized what a great miracle this was, they wondered if this was the one they had been expecting to come. They were about ready to take Jesus by force and make Him their king, their earthly king, when He took off. Yes, He did! He knew he was not to be an earthly king. He went up high into the mountains to escape, and He went alone. This crowd of people started looking for Jesus. They knew that He had not left with His disciples, because they saw them leave in a boat by themselves without Him.

The next morning, the crowds started gathering on the shore to wait for Jesus to come back down from the mountains. When He didn't come down, they decided to find Him. They sure did! They got into small boats and went to the other side of the lake to look for Him. When they got there, they saw that Jesus was there with His disciples. They asked Him how He had gotten there.

His disciples had quite a story to tell about that. They told how they were out in the boat when a great and violent wind came up. The sea was getting rough and rising high, and then they saw Jesus walking on the sea and approaching the boat. They were terrified! They thought He was a ghost. Thankfully, Jesus identified Himself. He called out to them, told them not to be afraid, and then they knew it was Him. Now here is the picture. He was walking on water (that is miraculous enough in itself), but that's not all. It was during a terrible wind with the water of the sea getting rough and high, so terrible they called it *violent*. So that's how He got there. He walked on the rough and high water during a terrible and violent wind to get to the boat. It was a miracle!

When these people that He had fed the night before arrived on the shore, Jesus knew what they were thinking before they ever said the first word! He knew even more than that. He knew their hidden motives, and He told them about it! He told them the truth, which wasn't pretty. No, it wasn't. He said He knew they wanted to be with Him just because He fed them, not because they believed in Him.

Oh, yes! He knows all about us. He knows when men are lying and what their hidden motives are. It is no use to try to manipulate Him or to trap Him either. Many tried and failed. He knows that too. Jesus tells the truth, no matter whom He is with. He is not scared of anyone or anybody. Nobody can bully Him.

Have you heard Him speak? He teaches with such power and authority! Did you know that He heals the sick with the touch of His hands or with the words of His mouth? It's true!

It was hard for Jesus to have any privacy at all. People were always seeking Him out to find Him. He was in a house one day when men got on the roof. There was such a crowd at the door of this house they couldn't get in. They couldn't get in by the door, but that didn't discourage them. No, siree, they did not give up! They carried with them a mat that contained a man who could not walk. They wanted Jesus to heal Him. They let this man down through the roof to get to this great healer and miracle worker. The man was healed, got off his mat, and walked out.

Jesus was popular for a short time. People came by the thousands to hear Him. Many of them had hopes of being healed by Him. One lady, who had been very sick for a long time, thought if she could just get close enough to Him to touch His clothes, then she would be healed. It happened for her (Luke 8:43–48)!

I cannot imagine what it would have been like to actually see Jesus, the one who was doing all of these unbelievable things. How many miles would I have traveled to be close to Him? I probably would have constantly heard new stories about Him. I would have been amazed to say the least. If I ever did get close to Him, I think I would have wanted to stay in His presence.

Well, it happened for me.

JESUS CAME
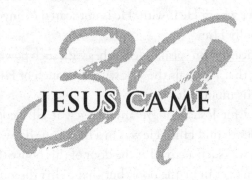

He came to me on a day that I was feeling crushed by my own sins and also by the sins of the county I live in. Yes, this is true.

Romans 3:23 (NIV):
"For all have sinned (Who? All of us.)
and fall short (Short of what?)
of the glory of God,
and are justified freely (Justified and it's free? By what?)
by His Grace (How?)
through the redemption (Through being redeemed?)
that came by (Whom?)
Christ Jesus."

Let's get this straight. So all of us are sinners. Yes. It's pretty simple. We all fall short of the glory of God, but by the grace of God, Jesus took care of those sins at the cross. We are justified, which means being made righteous in the sight of God. It is free to us because He redeemed us! He bought us back! He paid the price. The price was His life. We are paid for in full if we want to receive this beautiful grace from God.

Okay, I knew this in my head. This was not news to me. I had known it ever since I was ten years old. However, I didn't know what sin *felt* like to be on me. I had never felt the burden of sin lying on me in its evilness as I did that particular day. I was experiencing what was happening to me at that time and in that place when God opened my spiritual eyes to the sins that were around me and in me. It was awful. It was ominous. I sat in my favorite seat in our living room in a terrible shape. The feelings of sinfulness were dark and horrible and crushing. They were beyond heavy—dark, horrible, crushing, and heavy; I didn't feel equipped to carry them ... not at all. It was so bad I didn't see how I could go on living under all this pressure I was feeling from this ominous burden.

There was so much debate about the field parties. There seemed to be a decision to make of whether or not to stop a local park from having them anymore. I already felt beat up by the paper, and now I felt as if Jeremy and Amanda were being used as targets for this debate. There was so much going on that I felt crushed by it. Our county was being bombarded by opinions from both sides of this debate, and I felt as though it was all over me, covering me inside and out. We know that debates can be a healthy way for us to communicate our differences, but this one was stirring up trouble because of strong, rampant emotions from both sides. The emotions of passion, fear, pain, love, anger, and compassion were all mixed together. Was it going to divide our county? There were pointing fingers, backlashing, and word fighting only because each side felt they were right, as we all do when we are fighting for a cause. There was much fear from parents about losing more of our children if these gigantic, uncontrolled parties continued. The fight was on.

I felt that all of it was crushing me. You know what it means to crush something. It was as though I was being squeezed with great force and pounded and pounded. I even wanted to raise my arm physically to shield myself from all this stone throwing, all this anguish. This caused me to feel that I was suffocating in it. My lungs couldn't take it. The sins of our county, my sins included, were all over me. Now don't get me wrong. I love the county I live in. It has been home to me all my life and more than likely always will be. Don't know that for sure because I don't know the future, but I do love living here. I love the people of this county. It wasn't just about other people either; it was about my sins too. It was about sins, sins, sins. This was something that God wanted to show me. God allowed me to *feel* sin, and it was almost unbearable. I know that we feel, see, and live the consequences of sin, but I had never in my life ever felt sin all over me in this way. This was different. It was a nightmare. I wanted to break out of it and couldn't.

As I was suffering with this, *Jesus came*! I feel choked up just writing that sentence. It was most powerful. Believe me, I came to full attention. I felt His mighty presence. I knew He was standing right beside me! I didn't see Him or hear an audible voice, but He was there all the same! I will never forget the spot where His feet were planted in my living room. His presence brought calm, peace, and assurance. He had something He wanted to tell me.

He showed me the world as we see it when we look at a globe. As I looked at this globe He was holding in His hands, He wanted to show me a comparison. He worked to pinpoint the county that I live in on this globe and wanted me to see it. The dot was so microscopic that it could not even be seen with my human eyes. I just knew it was there, and I knew what He was doing. I nodded my head.

He wanted me to know that here is where I live on this great planet Earth, and even though it seems microscopic in comparison to the whole Earth, that doesn't matter. It is still a very significant place. It is just as important as any other place on the entire Earth. It was important for me to understand that.

He showed me that I had been *allowed* to see spiritually and to feel physically my own sins and the sins of everyone around me in this community of one county, so that I would understand the awfulness of sin and how horrible it is in itself. He wanted me to know that it is not only like this where I live, but it is like this everywhere on earth. We can't get away from sin.

Before He went any further in teaching me, He acknowledged that He knew I felt crushed by it, and He sympathized with how I was feeling. I felt His compassion for my suffering with it.

And then in his gentle way, he pointed out a huge difference between my pain and his pain. After he pointed to my location on the earth, he took his hand and moved it over the whole globe, in and around the whole earth. The difference in my pain and his pain was the fact that he had taken the sins of the whole world on his shoulders. He explained that I was only feeling a microscopic pinch of that pain and agony from my little world of one little county.

Oh my, my, my, my! My eyes were opened wide. There was no way that I could even begin to comprehend the magnitude of this comparison that He was explaining to me. Even though I knew He had taken all the sins with Him when they nailed Him to the cross, it was startling to understand just a pinch of what that *felt* like. I was *terrified* at the thought of Him taking the whole world's sins on Himself and what that felt like to Him!

"Oh, Jesus, how did you do it?"

It was then that understanding flooded my soul and sank into my brain. Oh, no! Oh, no! Oh, no! I knew what happened! I just knew it!

"Oh, Jesus, it killed you, didn't it?"

"Oh, Jesus, I can't imagine the pain and agony you suffered.

"Oh, Jesus," I cried. "It wasn't just the nails in your hands and the nails in your feet and hanging on that cross that killed you, was it? That was part of it, I know. Your physical body was sacrificed in pain and shed blood. Now I know more. It was the crushing weight of the sins of humankind that actually broke your heart and killed you, wasn't it? You died before the thieves did, right? They did not have to break your bones to help the death process. You were already dead."

> Now it was the day of Preparation, and the next day was to be a special Sabbath. Because the Jews did not want the bodies left on the crosses during the Sabbath, they asked Pilate to have the legs broken and the bodies taken down. The soldiers therefore came and broke the legs of the first man who had been crucified with Jesus, and then those of the other. But when they came to Jesus and found that he was already dead, they did not break his legs. Instead, one of the soldiers pierced Jesus' side with a spear, bringing a sudden flow of blood and water. (John 19:31–33 NIV)

"Dear Lord, God Almighty, I praise your holy name!" Thanksgiving flowed from me, and I fell to my knees in adoration to Jesus Christ the Lord. He is the Lamb. He is the Lamb of God, the sacrificial Lamb. He took the horrible, dark, evil sins of the whole wide world. They fell on His entire body in all their evilness, and they *crushed* Him!

They crushed His shoulders.
They crushed His back.
They crushed His heart.
They crushed His lungs.
They crushed His chest.
They crushed every tissue and cell of His entire body.

He gave His entire body. It was broken! Broken! Broken! It was broken by the crushing, suffocating sins of the whole wide world. His blood poured out of Him for all those sins. His blood poured out, and the sins poured out with the blood. There is power in His broken body and power in His shed blood. That's why the bread and the wine of Communion are so powerful.

"And he took bread, gave thanks and broke it, and gave it to them, saying, 'This is my body given for you; do this in remembrance of me.' In the same way, after the supper he took the cup, saying, 'This cup is the new covenant in my blood, which is poured out for you'" (Luke 22:19–20 NIV).

They crucified Him, not having a clue of the powerful magnitude of His broken body and His shed blood. They crucified Him, not knowing what they were doing. In fact, he said that while He was hanging there on the cross (Luke 23:34 NIV).

But it was the Father's plan that it happen in just this way. And then I thought, *There's even more!* I thought how He took the sins of ages past, of those of the present, and of those in the future! I had to take a deep breath. I was only experiencing what sin felt like in my own little life in my own little community in a few present moments before Jesus came that day. He didn't let me feel it for very long because it was more than I could bear! It was more than I could stand physically, mentally, and emotionally.

"Oh, Lord, the magnitude of this is more than I can comprehend. No wonder the world turned dark for three hours. The dark, evil sins were coming in on Jesus. No wonder you sweat great drops of actual blood in the Garden of Gethsemane. Your body was already breaking down with the agony. You were already feeling this evil, this ominous burden on you. No wonder you cried out for God to take it away from you while you were praying. Even though you knew this was what you came to earth to do, it was so crushing, heavy, dark, and evil that you could hardly stand it in your human body. No wonder an angel from heaven appeared to you and strengthened you! Oh, Lord, it was more than you could bear without some heavenly help, and God, your Father, knew it and sent the angel's help right away. You saw the angel with your eyes, and the angel gave you strength to go on. Oh, Jesus, you didn't give up, did you? Your mind, your heart, your soul were still in God's will. It brings tears to my eyes, gratefulness to my heart, and love from the depths of my soul."

"'Father, if you are willing, take this cup from me; yet not my will, but yours be done.' An angel from heaven appeared to him and strengthened him. And being in anguish, He prayed more earnestly, and his sweat was like drops of blood falling to the ground" (Luke: 22:42–44 NIV).

"Oh, Jesus, Father God did not rescue you from this, even though it pained Him so to see you suffer. Oh my! Oh my! Oh my!" I doubled over in pain. I knew God saw all and felt all, but now I had more of an idea of God the Father's suffering. He was suffering from it too, wasn't He? I felt that I was choking when this truth pushed through my consciousness. It was truth in a deeper level than I had ever known before. Father God was suffering in so many ways while Jesus, His one and only begotten Son was on that cross! I wanted to sob in compassion for Father God as He watched His Son take on all the evil of the world right on His own body. Father God was feeling every bit of it too, plus suffering for His Son.

Oh, the pain!

Oh, the agony!

Oh, the victory!

The Holy Trinity *together* broke Satan's power over us and won the war when Jesus gave His body and poured out His blood for all of us! It was so hard that no other human being could have done it. Jesus was the only one who could do it. He was God's only Son. It was difficult; it was so much suffering, but they did it anyway … for us! They did it for us! They did it for you; they did it for me.

Why?

Because that's how much they love us.

How can I comprehend love of this magnitude? Oh, my Lord, my precious Lord.

Then Jesus told me to let go of those sins that were on me. He said they weren't mine. Wow! He said they didn't belong to me. Let them go. Let them go. Let them go. He told me to let them go and give them to Him. They were His. They belonged to Him. He took care of sins and still takes care of sins.

And so I did. I let it all go, and I gave it all to Him.

I felt relief immediately.

I felt gratitude wash all over me.

I felt saved.

I felt safe from the evil that is on this earth. I knew it had been the evil one who had put all of this on me. The evil was gone when I gave it to Jesus.

I felt loved beyond measure.

And then Jesus left!

Oh no, no, no!

I begged him not to leave. I cried out loud, "Jesus, Jesus, please stay, please come back." I said this over and over.

He did not come back.

I was alone again.

I was alone to ponder just what had happened.

I sat in amazement of how well I knew Jesus. It was the same feeling I had had with Mary. I felt that I had always known Him. He was family!

I basked in this, and I realized more fully how He has been with me ever since I invited Him into my heart. He knows me inside and out, every detail. Even though His presence that He had made known to me had left, I knew that He was still with me, always living in my heart. The Holy Spirit will never leave me.

And then the grief set in. Oh, yes, it did! I missed His presence so much, and it was *awful*. I wanted him back just as I wanted Jeremy back. It was the same feeling, the same longing, the same grief. Yes, it was. I started begging and pleading for Him to come in His presence to see me again. This went on for days. But He didn't come back. The grief stayed, and I again understood Mary wanting her baby back even though she knew He was the Son of God. It didn't matter. She just wanted her baby back. Spiritually, she knew who Jesus was, but physically she felt the agonizing pain of being apart. I wanted Him back because He is my Savior, my friend, my brother, my family!

It was back to trusting Him again, knowing that He is always with me, and I finally accepted this. I felt humbled by His visit and by the comparison of my pain compared to His. I felt loved and cherished when He acknowledged my pain. He knew this was important to me emotionally. It is always important to acknowledge others in their pain as well. Pain of any kind is supposed to be acknowledged, not ignored. How can it heal if it is not acknowledged and loved? Love heals pain. Jesus acknowledged my pain and then asked me to give it to Him. He wanted to take care of it for me. He did not want me to carry this great pain. What can I say? This is too magnificent for words! Giving everything to Him released the gift of peace that passes all understanding.

Back to the debate over the field parties: the ruling came. They were stopped.

There were to be no more field parties. It was obvious that God was still in control.

Part VII

LIFE GOES ON

THE KODAK MOMENT

I saw Jeremy one more time. I call it my Kodak moment. He was so happy in this picture. It is there in the picture gallery of my mind along with the picture of him that I saw in my dream, and they are both there to stay.

It was six months after his death when I began to feel the urge to work in church again. God was prodding me, but I really didn't want to do it. I was scared. I felt weak. I just didn't know if I even had the energy to do it. After all, I still was having trouble sitting through an entire church service. How was I going to work in church? But the nudging would not go away.

I had gone back to work at school, which was difficult, and I just wanted to stay in my comfort zone. However, when God wants us to do something, He doesn't leave us alone. I knew in my heart what He wanted me to do, so I finally decided to give it a try. Why not? That was the least I could do. If it didn't work, I would give the position up. This was what was rolling around in my mind. But still, I was holding back a little. Did I want to let go of the reserve I had about it? The job was being the chairperson of our education committee. It involved being in charge of the Sunday school program, classes, teachers, materials, and so on. I had been offered the position and was hedging of course. I decided to go to a meeting where they were making these decisions, and I would give my answer.

The Holy Spirit was urging me to say yes, so I did. In fact, I couldn't hold it back while I was there! It spewed out of my mouth before my mind had time to catch up with it. I don't think a freight train could have held it back!

I drove home thinking about what I had done. Of course, that is when the doubts, fears, and regrets came crashing in on me, and I kept asking myself, "Why in the world did I do that?"

I opened the door to walk in the kitchen, and that is when Jeremy flashed before me, right there in the kitchen!

I was stunned!

It happened in an instant, and this is what I saw.

Happiness! He was bursting with happiness!

All those things I saw in him in the other picture were there along with a special something he was holding out to me. The special something was his joy. He was joyful that I had taken the position. This joy abounded everywhere around him, through him, and in him. It was fantastic!

He was real to me as I stood there in the kitchen watching him. And then, all of a sudden, I felt it too. This joy came inside of me. I knew that I had done what God wanted me to do when I said yes.

I have felt this joy as I have written this book. I know I am doing the work God wants me to do, and it is wonderful, joyful, and peaceful beyond all understanding.

I will never forget what I call Jeremy's Kodak moment. It was a picture flashed from heaven, sent to earth, and frozen in time in my mind.

"Thank you, oh, God. You never cease to amaze me!"

> But the fruit of the Spirit is love, joy, peace,
> patience, kindness, goodness,
> faithfulness, gentleness, and self-control.
> —Galatians 5:22 (NIV)

WORKING AT SCHOOL

I was an instructional assistant at the elementary school when Jeremy died. The accident happened in May, which was two weeks away from summer vacation. The principal, Mr. Cheek, came to visit me a few days after the funeral. He told me I didn't have to finish out the remaining two weeks of the school year. The employees had graciously given me days to compensate the pay. I didn't have to go back to work until the new school year started again. I was really relieved and quite thankful to these wonderful people. I truly live in a community of love. Their love still touches my heart even after all these years.

When time came to go back, I suffered many disturbances. It was Jeremy's elementary school. He had been the student of nearly all the teachers. It was the gym he had played in, the outside playground that he romped on with other children. There were reminders everywhere I turned.

It was then that I learned the power of a smile. Many smiled at me every time they saw me. The smiles were ever so strengthening. I couldn't believe the power that each smile had! They did not have to say a word, because their smiles told me everything I needed to know. As I write this, I am reaching for a Kleenex. Tears are flowing and blurring my vision. It still is so touching to me. How can genuine smiles have so much power? Those smiles were wonderful, tremendously encouraging, and healing. I had not known that a genuine smile has healing power in it, but it sure does!

It was at that time too that words became more beautiful and powerful to me than ever before. I could now absorb words, whereas before I couldn't. They had more healing balm in them or they had more pain in them, but mostly I received healing balm from gracious and loving people. As I saw many people at school, including the staff, the children, and the parents, and as I met people around town, their words became living things to me. Some of my favorites were these:

"I'm so glad to see you."

"I pray for you every day."

"You are on my mind."

"I love you."

Such beautiful, healing words! I was grateful for every one of them.

We also had received and were still receiving many cards, letters, and notes. I read them over and over again. I took those words into my heart, and I could look at them anytime I wanted to. They had the power to sustain and encourage me. All of these were important to my healing process. Written words were very powerful to me because I could see them with my eyes, hear them with my ears, soak them into my soul, and read them anytime I wanted to. Smiles and words were my encouragers and helped to hold me up from day to day. They were born out of love, and love is strengthening and healing to the soul.

Then the anger set in again. I wanted to bash everything in sight. I had the desire to knock out every window in that building. Of course, I knew I couldn't do that, so I started smashing them in my mind. I smashed everything in sight. My imagination took over and mentally helped me to vent, vent, vent.

As I have mentioned before, I was angry when I went to the cemetery. I wanted to kick that headstone as hard as I could. I cried, "Why did you leave me, Jeremy?" I was mad at Jeremy for leaving me. I was mad at myself for not taking better care of him. That is what parents are supposed to do, and I had failed. And then here it came. I was mad at God too. I was mad at him for not intervening and saving Jeremy and Amanda. I was mad at the world and everything in it.

There was nothing to do except to feel the anger and vent it in my mind, which helped when I had to keep control of myself at work. It helped to recognize the anger, not squelch it but give it the dignity it deserved. I battled with it for quite some time. When I was home, I would beat the floor with my fists, cry out loud, letting it out. Letting anger out in healthy ways was very healing. It finally was spent and was gone.

Another dilemma I was having at school was the fact that all the little boys looked like Jeremy. They would look up at me, and all I could see was his face. The days became long and painful. It was a relief to get in the car to come home. However, there was another torment waiting for me there. As soon as I started the car and headed out, the same record started playing in my head. "Jeremy was killed last night. Jeremy was killed last night." On and on and on, it played just like a stuck record. Tears streamed down my face as I tried to control myself enough to get to my house. I would fall in the kitchen door and let it out. Groaning, moaning, weeping, whatever came out of me was a relief. I would collapse on the couch until it was all out. Wave after wave of grief consumed me until it was spent; then a new day started it all over again.

It got worse. I felt as if I was walking in mud up to my waist to just get in the doorway at the school. It felt that the mud was so heavy I could barely lift my feet. I struggled to get in. I struggled to walk down the halls. I struggled to work with the children.

I loved the people I worked with. They treated me with such love and kindness that wrapped around me like a blanket of comfort. I loved them a lot. I loved the little children that I worked with. I wanted my emotional state to get better. I wanted the torment to end.

I worked at school for three more years, but it was taking its toll on me. I felt that I had given work sufficient time for me to get better, but I hadn't. I knew that I needed to move on, so I turned in my resignation.

> But You, O God, do see trouble and grief;
> you consider it to take it in hand.
> —Psalm 10:14

43

GRIEVING PARENTS

Billy and I grieved together and grieved separately too. Each person grieves in his or her own way. It was very important that we respect each other's way of grieving. It was very important for us to work together on this. We had a lot of daily decisions to make, and there would be days, when something would come up that would make him feel worse but make me feel better. Then there would be days when there were things that would come up that might make him feel better but make me feel worse. We worked hard on being considerate of each other's grief. We had a rule that we abided by. If it would make one feel better but make the other feel worse, we simply would not do it. The last thing in the world we wanted to do was make it worse for either one of us. It was bad enough without adding to it.

We drew up Jeremy's headstone together. We decorated the grave together. It took a year before we could go to the place where the accident happened. We waited until we were both ready. It also took a year before we could go into Jeremy's room and sort through his belongings. The door to his room had stayed shut. When we did go in there, it was for short periods of time. It took longer than that before we actually worked with Jeremy's clothes. Each step we took together was only when both of us were ready. We honored each other in our separate grief. The pain we each endured was great. We both had lots of support, love, and encouragement from many who loved and cared about us. We helped each other for eight years in every way possible.

I have to share something else with you. It was during these years that there was one tragedy after another. There were *seventeen* boys who died from different circumstances. Jeremy knew *every one* of these boys. They were his friends. It is true. This really happened. It was hard to believe it was happening, but it was. There were many of them whose parents were our friends. In fact we had been friends with some of those parents our whole adult lives and sometimes even from childhood. We had watched each other's children grow up. The pain from all of this was excruciating. It was awful. We grieved with them and for them. It was so hard because we also knew what pain was ahead for all these parents. There just aren't any words to convey what we felt for all of them. We loved them and their children, still do. I am not going to name names, but if any of you parents are reading this book, you know I am talking about you and your precious children. My heart is with you and always has been.

Of course, tragedies haven't stopped. In the last twenty years, there have been even more children to die that we know, and our hearts go out to every family that has to endure the pain and anguish.

God knows our pain. His Son died too. And He is with us in our grieving.

MADELYN

Something very exciting happened on December 13, 1999. Our granddaughter was born! This was wonderful! Madelyn Shane Burns came into our lives and brought us much happiness. Her middle name is Shane, same as Jeremy's middle name. We were there in the delivery room minutes after she was born. I'll never forget those first moments of seeing her. Again, I felt those grandmother feelings that come when a grandbaby is born. These are those feelings that can't even be described with words. At least, I have found no words for it!

When Madelyn was a week old, Dustin came down with the flu. The doctor did not want Madelyn to be around the flu virus, so Madelyn stayed with us for a week. I know this was very hard on Julie, Brian and Dustin. Anyway, she slept in her little baby seat or on a pallet on the floor, and I slept on the couch right beside her. The nights were very interesting. I had forgotten how many little baby noises there actually are! I think she used all the baby vocabulary while she slept!

I became Madelyn's part-time babysitter when Julie went back to work as a dental secretary. Madelyn and I got along great. We talked a lot even though she couldn't talk! Before she could sit up on her own, I would prop her up in the corner of the couch, look into her eyes, and ask her questions! She would look back at me with those big, beautiful eyes she has, and I knew she was trying to translate my questions. We communed together in everything we did. Oh, yes we did! I felt bonded with her in such a mighty and powerful way and still do. This little girl was another Godsend to me. Thank you, God, for Madelyn!

Julie and Brian moved into a new house that Brian and his father, Travis, had built together. Dustin was about five years old at the time, and Madelyn was close to a year old. I kept Madelyn during the day, and Dustin would come to our house after kindergarten until Julie got off work. Anyway, one day at their new house, someone had left the basement door opened, and Julie didn't know it. Madelyn thought she would check it out and rolled all the way down the basement steps. Julie rushed to pick her up, but she was just fine. Diaper padding had helped with the fall. Madelyn was in better shape than Julie! I knew in my heart that Jeremy was smiling, knowing that Madelyn was okay. Thank you, Lord, for taking care of Madelyn.

I took her to visit my grandmother, Moma Eva, about once a week. Moma Eva couldn't see her. She had lost her sight, but she enjoyed our visits very much. This was before Madelyn could walk, so she just sat in my lap and watched and listened to everything we said and did.

Oh how quickly Madelyn grew up! I remember we were having a yard sale when Madelyn was six or seven years old. She played around in the yard singing at the top of her lungs. Her favorite song to sing at that time was, "I've Been Working on the Railroad." She belted it out, enjoying every minute of it. Moma Eva would have loved to have heard her singing because Moma Eva loved to hear people sing. She had already passed on when Madelyn started singing, but she would have been very happy about it if she were still here. Moma Eva didn't care anything about watching TV or listening to the radio. She liked real live music! When she was older, Madelyn sang in church and also sang a song on our local radio station. She sang a solo at her basketball Parents' Night too. But back to when she was five, six, seven, years old, Madelyn would put on Moma Eva's slips that I kept when she passed away, and she would pretend they were her evening gowns. She would look for women's slips to buy when she went to yard sales so she would have several different kinds of evening gowns! Then she would wear them over her clothes when she went out to visit people and visit yard sales!

In 2005, I moved into Moma Eva's house, and when Madelyn stayed all night with me, we would sleep in a bedroom that had stairs in it that led to the upstairs. When we would go to bed, Madelyn would be afraid of the steps and the upstairs. We would whisper, and I would tell her not to be afraid because upstairs was a wonderful place at night! I told her there were young, beautiful angels up there, and they were all wearing sparkly evening gowns of all different colors. She would want to know why they were there. I would tell her they were there to watch over us during the night. She would want me to describe their gowns, and that would put her right to sleep! During the day, we would go upstairs, and she would play dress up with my dresses, hats, scarves, and purses.

Madelyn loved to dance. We would put on aerobic dancing tapes and whirl away, or turn on the radio, or put in CDs and sing as loud as we could, jumping and dancing until we fell down exhausted. As you can guess, I always ran down before she did. We know how that works! When Dustin was eight or nine years old, he would waltz with Madelyn (she was four or five) to music, and it was the cutest sight ever.

We have experienced a lot of life together so far, and I look forward to what is ahead. It is hard to believe that Madelyn is a junior at Nelson Co. High. She spent one summer babysitting her cousins Tanner and Breckin. She got her driver's license this spring. She spent this past summer working at our local mill that makes wonderful flour, meal, and spices. She stays active playing volleyball and is always on the go. She goes to volleyball camp in the summers at Morehead College. She loves dressing up for all the dances at school. She goes to church camps and retreats. She is good at basketball too and loves dogs. She likes to read and be with her friends. She is wonderful, compassionate, funny, and direct. I love going in her room and watching movies together. We laugh hard and sometimes cry if the movies are sad. We have the best time. We are friends as well as family.

Madelyn has had a lot of grief in her life. She watched as her Pappaw Travis suffered and died with stomach cancer. He adored her, and she adored him. It was anguish for her. Dustin and Madelyn both grieved immensely for their grandfather. She has stayed with her Mammaw Janet a lot since his passing so she won't be alone. She is very close to her Mammaw Janet and loves her very much.

Dustin and Madelyn had a good friend, Joe, who died unexpectedly. They loved him so much. There have been many other serious issues that she has had to deal with. She has come through them with great determination and strong faith. I told her one time that I knew she had been through so much grief in her short life, and I knew it had all been so hard on her. I wanted to acknowledge her pain and tell her how I felt about it. She agreed. She continually moves on. Dustin has shared in all these painful issues. His strong faith in God has shown him, led him, and comforted him through it all. God is with them both. God never promised that things would run smoothly down here on earth. He promises though that He will see us through it and never leave us as orphans in it.

Grandchildren are such gifts from above. Grandparents and grandchildren are such gifts to each other! Dustin and Madelyn are on my mind, in my heart, and welded in my soul. I love them both so much. They are a part of me, and I am a part of them. My life goes on through them, and I watch in fascination. Generations come and go, and how beautiful they are! What a great link we have to those who have gone before us in generations past and with those who go after us. We are a never-ending circle of love and life. There is always something to look forward to through them because we will all live forever and will always be!

I know that Jeremy watches over Madelyn and protects her. I know that he gets a real kick out of her bubbly, energetic, ever-moving life. I know he has enjoyed watching her grow up and loves her tremendously. I know she makes him smile and probably laugh too!

> Children's children are a crown to the aged, and
> parents are the pride of their children.
> —Proverbs 17:6 (NIV)

OUT OF THE BLUE

You know what happens just when we think we have life figured out? It changes. It's just the way life is. For years, I didn't see how life could go on without Jeremy, but God made a way to push us forward. Just as the sun came up every morning and set in the evening, it continually moved us and continues to move us to a new day. Grief does not stop time, and it does not stop other things from happening.

When Jeremy died, I knew my life would never be the same. How could it be? Life changed at that time, and it has continued to change. In fact, it has changed so much it has been hard for me to keep up with it. People, circumstances, situations, challenges, crossroads, you name it, all keep coming at me from out of the blue. The thing I know for certain is the fact that God has used every person, every circumstance, every situation, every challenge, and every crossroad for the good in my life. It has been lots of hard work, loads of hard knocks, more grief, and lots of living and learning. There have also been good things, wonderful experiences, and happy times. There have been the valleys and the mountains. In all of it, God never ceases to amaze me. Some of these things are expected, and some of them arrive out of the blue. That's been my life. I know without a shadow of a doubt though that God was not surprised by any of it. I have made a lot of mistakes. He has disciplined me through them, and He has enriched me through them. I love Him so.

"Out of the blue" is very precious to me. When Jeremy was fifteen or so years old, he said to me one time, "You know, Mom, you all never give me anything out of the blue. I just wish you would."

I'll never forget it. I just looked at him and really didn't know what to say. I had never ever thought of something like that.

A few months after he died, I went to the post office to get stamps one day, and there sitting on the counter were new note cards and envelopes for sale that said, "Out of the Blue."

I froze.

I couldn't quit staring at them.

I remember thinking, *What is going on here?*

There they were, big as you please, right there on the counter where you buy stamps!

Of course I had to buy them!

I knew Jeremy was speaking to me, and I knew I was supposed to send them to people so they would get something out of the blue.

Life is precious and ever changing in the small and the large events of our lives. Good things and hard things both can be changes from out of the blue. Some things we plan to change, but some things are not our doing. Change happens. God is still in control, always has been and always will be. We don't have to be in control; in fact, it is impossible. There will be presents from out of the blue—notes, gifts, flowers, phone calls, visits, cards, fun, laughter, good times, all the good stuff. There will also be changes that affect our lives deeply. Living life down here doesn't mean that we are going to be happy all the time. That's just not going to happen. But we will grow spiritually during our happy and our unhappy times when we give these times to the Lord. James tells us about this very thing.

James 1:2–4 (NIV):
"Consider it pure joy, my brothers, (When?)
whenever you face trials of many kinds, (Say what? Joy when I face trials? Give me a break, James!)
because you know (I know what?)
that the testing of your faith (Ouch—that testing hurts!)
develops perseverance. (What does that mean? I looked it up. It means ... staying power! I must hang in there with the Lord no matter what!)

(Sorry James, I interrupted you. What about perseverance?)
Perseverance must finish its work (Oh, okay. Why?)
so that you may be mature and complete, (Oh, that sounds good!)
not lacking anything." (Oh how great that will be!)

James wants me to count it all as joy when all these changes have come into my life and turned everything upside down and I hurt so badly I can hardly stand it? Did I get that right? Of course, some of these changes are my own fault, but I don't deliberately set out to make mistakes, fall on my face, make bad decisions, and cause my own unhappiness. But it does happen. And James wants me to be joyful about it?

Well, Peter said the same thing only in a different way!

1 Peter 1:6–7 (NIV):
"In this you greatly rejoice, though now for a little while you may have had to suffer grief in all kinds of trials. (Suffer?)
These have come (Why?)
so that your faith—
of greater worth than gold, (Faith must be priceless!)
which perishes even though refined by fire—(Faith gets run over sometimes.)
may be proved genuine (It's the real stuff.)
and may result in praise, glory, and honor (It's worth it all.)
when Jesus Christ is revealed." (Praise His name.)

Trials, tribulations, and testings help us to become genuine in our faith. James and Peter both had more than their fair share of changes, trials, and grief in their lifetimes. They are definitely talking from experience! They became stronger because of these trials. If I listen to James and Peter, I can remember that these changes we go through that are sorrowful are only for a little while, whether they are because of our own fault or something beyond our control. They will change again because God can turn them into something that is of greater worth than gold! He reminds us that our genuine faith through it all may result in praise, glory, and honor going to God. He offers forgiveness, grace, and comfort. He offers whatever is needed.

Grief is as much a part of our ever-changing lives as anything else in our lives. Suffering is deep. We are remade during suffering, and God will continually send us reassurances from out of the blue.

Below is part of a speech I gave one time. The ladies had asked me to talk about change, so the title of my speech was simple: "Life Is about Change." I had been making notes for my message each day leading up to the day of the speech. One day I had a wonderful experience. God spoke to me about change. This is what happened:

> I was picking apples off the tree last week
> When God spoke to my heart,
> And He said to my spirit,
> "*Enjoy* picking these apples.
> This is a blessed moment in time that you should cherish."
> Well, that sure came from out of the blue!
> I sure hadn't expected God to talk to me
> When I was picking apples!
> At the time, I had been picking apples mechanically,
> Not really thinking about the apples or the tree.
> After He said that,
> I stopped picking,
> And I got inside the tree.
> It felt *wonderful* in there.
> I looked up through the branches, the leaves, and the green apples.
> I just gazed up at their beauty for a while,
> And it really seemed to be a magical place I was in.
> I could hear other apples falling and hitting the ground.
> I felt truly blessed in that moment.
> I thought of how that apple tree goes through all kinds of changes
> To produce that beautiful ripe fruit.
> It fights the elements of the winter, the wind,
> freezing temperatures, snow, and ice.
> It comes alive in the spring with gorgeous blossoms
> That turn into little apples.
> It gives itself all summer to the work of producing ripe fruit.
> It becomes full of beauty in the fall

> But loses its beauty in the winter.
> It looks dead for a short while.
> It's only resting.
> It comes alive again in the spring
> And starts working on wonderful new fruit.
> God taught me about change
> In the moments of looking at
> And listening to the apple tree.
> It touched my soul deeply.
> And it all came from out of the blue!
>
> That's just like God to send a message from out of the blue!
> "Thank you, God!"

Every moment of our lives is important. God is in every minute. To produce the fruit of the Holy Spirit, who lives in us, we must be transformed through changes too. We may not feel joyful at the time of many changes, but we will reap joy in time if we stay connected to Him. We go through the springs, summers, falls, and winters of life, and then it starts all over again each year. I love the start of a new year. It seems like a new beginning. There is no way I can know what will come from out of the blue for the new year, but I know it will be a mix of happy and unhappy in the circumstances of life. It is really best that I do not know what is ahead. God gives me strength to deal with it as each thing happens and not before. One day I will be like the winter of the apple tree, but I will not be here to blossom in the spring here on earth. Things will change tremendously when that happens. My body will be dead, but my soul/spirit will have a new beginning in heaven. It may come from out of the blue when I take off for glory land with no warning, or I may know ahead that life is ending. Who knows? God knows. I will be like a new tree planted where there will be no unhappiness, no tears, no sorrow, and no problems. Oh what a glorious future to look forward to! Everything there will be magnificent and spectacular beyond our imagination for all of us who love the Lord. Change ... life is about change and changing.

I know there are some things in life that I can change with God's help; there are also things that He wants me to leave alone and put them in His hands. There is one thing I know that I should be changing on an ongoing basis, and that is me. I am supposed to be renewing my mind. I'm supposed to be working on that new creature that the Holy Spirit is creating inside of me and bring her out into this life of circumstances and change. We are supposed to change and grow continuously with the Holy Spirit leading. God never changes, Jesus never changes, the Holy Spirit never changes. They are perfect, and they are in us to help us grow into that perseverance (staying power) that leads to maturity and completeness. They help us be refined as we go through the fires of life. These things make our faith greater than any gold on earth. I can't change by myself, but I don't have to. I have all of heaven helping me.

It was ten o'clock one night, years ago, and I was standing in the middle of the kitchen eating Cheez-Its. Oh, they were good! As I munched on them, I had another treat from out of the blue.

God spoke to me and said, "You have nothing to worry about, not one thing."

My jaw dropped!

I said, "I don't?"

(I was thinking, *Are you sure?*)

(Of course He heard my thoughts. It's not like I could hide them!)

And then I repeated it back to myself, "I have nothing to worry about, not one thing."

I felt in my soul that it was true. God will take care of me in all things, great and small, through all the changes in my life.

Did this stop more pain from coming into my life?

No, it did not. But I know without a shadow of a doubt that he will always send me things from out of the blue to help me cope, no matter what happens. A lot of it comes right out of His Word ... the Holy Bible.

I have pondered this "out of the blue" because of when Jeremy said to me, "You know, Mom, you all never give me anything out of the blue; I just wish you would."

Life is wonderful when we give little surprises of things that others enjoy, or precious words that fill their souls with joy and love, or moments to remember. Surprises, words, and moments come from the gift of ourselves, and we can send them from out of the blue. All these things are priceless. It is powerful when God speaks things from out of the blue to us, His children, as He gives of Himself to us. What a great Father we have! He is always full of surprises from out of the blue, whether it be an unexpected, breathtaking rainbow, a surprise rain shower when it's dry, a tree growing out of a boulder, a baby's bursting out in laughter that goes on and on and gets everybody laughing, words spoken from Him when we least expect it ... the list is endless. I am more aware now of things from out of the blue.

These gifts are enormous.

Part VIII

HOME

ONE GOD

Jesus lived physically for thirty-three years. In that time, He did something that no other person has ever been able to do. He defeated Satan. He defeated Satan with His life, and with His death, and with His resurrection. He was human on His mother's side of the family, and He was divine from His Father, God. His miracles knew no bounds when He was alive here on earth, and they know no bounds from His throne in heaven. In Matthew 28:18, Jesus tells His disciples about His power. His Father has given Him all authority in heaven and earth. He is ruler over everything and everybody. The power is all His. He is King of Kings and Lord of Lords.

There are many different religions in the world today and always have been. They were started by men, not God. None of those men were the Son of the Living God. None of them fulfilled time's ancient prophecies during their lifetimes on this earth. None of them knew everything; they only knew some things. Jesus was the wisest person to walk on this earth. He knew everything. He was perfect. He was divine. He is the Son of God. He is the only one we are to worship.

God has given wisdom to a lot of people here on earth. He gave great wisdom to King Solomon, and he helped Solomon write some of the scriptures. We can learn a lot from him. However, King Solomon never made the claim that he had all the answers or was equal to God. In fact, he said just the opposite.

Solomon was King David's son and was to inherit his father's throne, so before King David died, he called Solomon in to give him some fatherly advice and guidance. David told Solomon to be strong and show himself to be a real man. The way to be a real man was to let God lead him in all His ways and to keep God's commandments. This was the greatest advice of all. King David was wise too. He told Solomon to walk with God in truth with all his heart, mind, and soul (1 Kings 2:1–4).

God appeared to Solomon in a dream one night and told him that he would give him whatever he asked for. Solomon asked for an understanding mind and a hearing heart, so that he could judge his people correctly between good and bad. Solomon was young. He knew he did not have the wisdom on his own to be a good king of Israel. God was pleased with what Solomon had requested and told him that he would give him a wise and discerning mind. In fact, there would not be any person who would ever rise to such heights of wisdom as Solomon! Solomon was a wise man; however, Solomon was not divine. Solomon was many things during his lifetime and was known all over for his great wisdom, riches, and power. He was a great king, judge, entrepreneur, teacher, preacher, poet, wise man, wealthy man, and so on. He continually searched for wisdom and meaning in life. He was a writer, and we have records in the Bible of his writings. From the book of Ecclesiastes, Solomon in all of his knowledge, wisdom, wealth, power, and searching says that nothing is truly new. History only repeats itself! He says he applied himself to searching for understanding about everything in the universe and found out the truth. It was futile business. No human has this ability. He said it was like chasing the wind.

He says what is wrong cannot be made right and there is no use in thinking what might have been. There is no use in looking back. (No use in thinking of the "if onlys!")

He tried searching for meaning in all worldly ways only to become discouraged about it. He decided to experience life to the fullest. He said He tried drinking and folly while sticking to his course of seeking wisdom and found no fulfillment with either one of them. He then started a great public works program, building homes, vineyards, gardens, parks, and orchards. He made reservoirs to hold water to irrigate his plantations. He had men and women slaves, great herds and flocks, silver and gold. He organized men's and women's choirs and orchestras. He had many beautiful wives and concubines. He evaluated all these things, and the answers were not there. He felt it was all foolishness. Why?

In his wisdom, he knew none of this was enough in itself. He decided it was best to enjoy life, whatever it may bring. He admitted that everything comes from the pleasure of God, and God has the right to deal with the world in any way He wants.

It is, after all, God's world. We have no peace apart from the true Living God, no matter what all we do or accomplish in life.

Solomon got discouraged at times because, in his wisdom, his eyes were opened to more wickedness as well as to the goodness on the earth. In this discouragement, he did admit that through it all, through the good and the bad, it is a wonderful thing to be alive. He says to rejoice in every day of life on earth. But remember that eternity is far longer and that everything down here is futile in comparison. Eternity is what really matters.

Even with all the wisdom that God gave him, Solomon still fell into sin. He was not above temptation. None of us are. Satan wanted Solomon too! Satan works on us all the time. This is part of our earthly existence. Solomon was far from perfect. There were false gods that humankind had made there in Solomon's day, and he fell into worshipping them, which was very sinful in God's sight.

Solomon says to be warned because there is no end to opinions from humankind! Humankind can come up with all kinds of ideas that are totally wrong. And it is so easy to fall right into them. Worshipping other gods was the wrong thing for Solomon to do, and he knew it.

In Acts 14:8–15, when Paul went on his missionary journeys and healed the sick in Jesus's name, he found that people would want to bow down and worship him. They thought he was a god in a human body! But Paul simply would not allow this. He knew it was wrong.

Neither would the angels allow this when someone would want to drop to their knees to worship them. They wouldn't allow it either, saying they were only God's servants. There is only one God to worship, who is our Creator and our Father, and his Son Jesus the Christ.

I found something very interesting as I was studying about Christ's death. It brought joy to my heart as the Holy Spirit pointed it out to me. I found it in John 19:38–42.

There were two men who wrapped Jesus's body for burial. Neither one of them was one of the twelve of the Lord's apostles. Both of these men had been secret followers. One was a man named Joseph of Arimathea. This man had been one of those secret followers of Jesus because he was afraid of the Jewish leaders. However, when Jesus died, fear didn't matter to Joseph of Arimathea anymore! It says he was very bold! He even asked Pilate if he could take Jesus's body down from the cross! Can you imagine the courage it took to go to the governor and ask for the body of Jesus? Wow! Pilate said that would be okay for him to do that.

Well, here is another interesting part for me. The other man who helped to embalm Jesus was Nicodemus. Oh my goodness! Yes! Nicodemus, the one who had come to Jesus at night to ask Him questions about who He was. Yes, Nicodemus, who wanted to know so badly that he waited until it was dark so no one would see him come to talk with Jesus. Yes, that Nicodemus! His fear didn't matter anymore either. It was gone. He didn't care who saw him.

Nicodemus brought one hundred pounds of embalming ointment made from myrrh and aloes. Now that's a lot of ointment! One hundred pounds of it! Together, he and Joseph of Arimathea prepared Jesus's body for burial.

Having buried a son, I know the very last thing we do for our loved one's bodies in preparing them to be laid to rest in death is a very precious thing to us and very dear to our hearts. This must have been very precious and dear to God's heart as He watched Joseph and Nicodemus take such loving care of His one and only Son's broken body. These two men weren't scared anymore! Perfect love casts out fear. Jesus had loved them perfectly. They publically showed their belief by lovingly taking care of Jesus's broken body; and not only that, it has been recorded so that the whole world can know that this is what they did. They were not afraid. They were not ashamed.

All that stuff just didn't matter anymore!

It's just as Jesus told Nicodemus about the Holy Spirit. It is like the wind. We have no control over the wind. We hear it. We feel its effects, but we can't tell where it comes from or where it's going. We do not know to whom the Holy Spirit will next bestow this life from heaven. Nicodemus and Joseph believed.

Jesus's last words on the cross were, "It is finished." He finished what He came to earth to do! He took care of that problem that happened in the Garden of Eden. We do not have to live in this sinful earthly state forever. That is over! His work is finished, but ours is not. God the Father, Jesus the Son, and the Holy Spirit will help us in our work. We have all of heaven on our side.

THE HOLY BIBLE

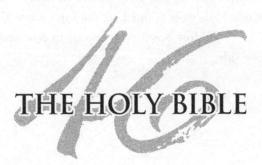

We were having a deep discussion about faith when my friend Cyndi mentioned she had read the Bible seven times from front to back. I just looked at her. I was so impressed. I didn't know what to say. Also, I was embarrassed to admit that I had never read the Bible completely, starting at the beginning and reading straight through to the end. Wow! I sat there amazed at what she said.

"Seven times, you say?"

"Yes," she said.

I still just looked at her.

Why haven't I read the Bible straight through even one time? I was silently asking myself.

Now, this is what I had done all my life. I had pulled out sections of it as needed. I knew the books of the Bible by heart. I knew the Old Testament stories. I knew how to look up and read whatever I wanted. I had been to countless Sunday school classes and learned lessons, read scripture passages, and memorized verses from childhood throughout adulthood. When I was a child, we had one of those huge Bibles with 8 x 10 colored pictures on one side and the story told on the other side. I absolutely loved them. As an adult, I was a Sunday school teacher and felt I knew the Bible pretty well. I had searched from here to there in it. I knew how to look up whatever I wanted.

I had done all these things, but never once had I picked up the Bible and read it straight through like a book. I had thought about it. But even as I thought about it, I would pick up another type of book and start reading it. *Another time*, I thought. *I will read it another time*, yet that other time had not come.

Also, I must confess, this was not the first time that this subject of reading the whole Bible had come up. Talking to Cyndi about this triggered my memory. I remembered my grandson, Dustin, asking me one time how many times I had read the whole Bible through. He thought I had read it multiple times! That too was embarrassing; well, really, it was even more than embarrassing. I also felt very, very small. I felt as small as a thimble, even smaller than that, because I felt as if I had crawled under that little thimble and was peeping out when I said in a very, very low voice, "None."

I knew he could barely hear me when I said it. He didn't say anything. Not one word. I felt smaller. I wondered what he was thinking. I could tell he was quite surprised. I did give myself a point for being honest though.

But I still didn't do it! I forgot about it in time.

However, this time her words went straight to my heart, and the memory of Dustin's asking me went straight to my heart, mind, and soul and was about to burn holes in them. I didn't feel small this time. I just knew it was time. I had the desire. I knew the Lord had put these people in my path to prompt me to read His book straight through from cover to cover and then gave me the desire to do it.

This is it, I thought. *No more putting it off, no more making excuses, no more picking up other books to read. I want to read the Bible from cover to cover, and I am going to do it.*

I started on January 1. It was one of my new year's resolutions. I was committed to reading the Bible all the way through from front to back. No skipping around, no pulling out, no going here and there.

I was using a Bible that had it already figured out how to read the Bible in one year. I followed its schedule for a while, and then I forgot about schedules. I just read and read.

I did it.

And I felt wonderful when I finished. I have always loved the Bible, but I had never felt this way before. I had never felt so complete, so awed, so blessed.

I held this book in my hands and praised God.

And I was speechless to say more. My heart was filled to overflowing, and there were no words to express the deep emotions of my soul.

"Thank You, Lord, for using Dustin and Cyndi to bring me to my knees in humbleness and pointing me in the right direction. I was very grateful and still am. I am glad I didn't miss the joy of reading the Holy Bible all the way through like I would read other books. It is the most important book in the whole world. We are so blessed to have it. Thank you, Father in heaven."

I'LL SEE YOU AT CHURCH IN THE MORNING!

Oh, how precious are the last words that Jeremy spoke to us on that last Saturday morning that he lived! As he walked out the kitchen door, he looked back at us and said, "I'll see you at church in the morning."

We said, "Okay."

We never doubted this for a minute. We knew he would be there.

But it didn't turn out that way. Jeremy went to another church on that fateful Sunday morning. He went to that place where the Lord God Almighty and Jesus are the temple. No walls of a building are needed. He went to that heavenly place that is impossible for us to even begin to imagine. When his spirit left his body, he was in the heavenly realm. He was never alone in death. He was greeted by angels. He was greeted by those loved ones of his who had gone on before him. His Pappaw Ockerman and Mom-maw Brown and all other relatives and friends were there waiting for him. He got to come face-to-face with the Lord Jesus.

In his poem to us that JoAnn wrote, Jeremy said that he had found that place he'd been searching for. We are all searching for that place because it is implanted in our souls. It is where we came from, and we long to be there because we belong there! It is available to all of us who want it. We are invited to come back!

"The Spirit and the bride say, 'Come!' And let him who hears say,

'Come!' Whoever is thirsty, let him come; and whoever wishes, let him take the free gift of the water of life" (Revelation 22:17 NIV).

Jeremy also told us in his poem that we wouldn't believe how bright the light is in heaven.

"I did not see a temple in the city, because the Lord God Almighty and the Lamb are its temple. The city does not need the sun or the moon to shine on it, for the glory of God gives it light, and the Lamb is its lamp" (Revelation 21:22–23 NIV).

Heaven's church is open to all of us who will receive the message of the Lamb of God who is Jesus Christ. The glory of God and his Son are the light of the world and the light of heaven. Jesus is the Lord of Lords and King of Kings, and He will reign forever. This is where Jeremy went to church on May 19, 1996.

"Yes, Jeremy, we will see you at church in the morning!"

48
JESUS IS COMING BACK

Jesus is coming back!

After His visit to me and we knew each other so well and I grieved for Him to come back, I am eagerly looking forward to being with Him again, not just in spirit but totally together. I know that day will come one way or another. It is in my future and your future. Oh, what joy we have to look forward to!

There are many things about Jesus's birth, life, death, and resurrection that were predicted throughout history. God told His prophets these things, and they in turn prophesized what was to come. These things are recorded in the Old Testament.

The actual occurring of these events happened. They were recorded in the New Testament in what we call the four Gospels—Matthew, Mark, Luke, and John. The book of Acts tells us how the church of Jesus Christ got moving with the fire and passion of the Holy Spirit. We can follow some of these new churches. We have their early history, and we can learn from their mistakes, failures, and victories and grow in knowledge and wisdom by studying the life of the Corinthians, Romans, Galatians, Ephesians, Philippians, and the Thessalonians. We learn from Peter, Paul, Timothy, Titus, James, John, and many more as we study the New Testament. They wrote it all down for us with the wind of the Holy Spirit moving through them. The apostle John wrote Revelation, the last book of the Bible. This book tells how the world is going to end, of the coming back of Jesus and the city of heaven. The Bible starts with the beginning of the earth and ends with the ending of it. It is astounding to me how the Old Testament and the New Testament come together in perfect unity! I know I have said that before, but it is new to me every time! Everything that was foretold about Jesus came to pass, from God's promise to Abraham to the end of Jesus's life. Even tiny details were prophesized, and they too came to pass! As I read the four Gospels, it amazes me how they all fit together. As I read the rest of the books, I am equally astonished how so many different writers knew how to take the Old Testament and explain it fully to unite with the New Testament into completion.

How did they do it?

Timothy tells us how they did it. He says all of the Holy Bible was written by the Holy Spirit of God, who breathed the scriptures in the author's hearts, minds, and souls. It was like the wind that came inside the writers."All scripture is God-breathed and is useful for teaching, rebuking, correcting and training in righteousness, so that the man of God may be thoroughly equipped for every good work" (2 Timothy 3:16 NIV).

God is fully aware of what we need, and He has supplied it for us. We have all we need right there in the Holy Bible, and we have the Holy Spirit as our personal guide to help us to understand and apply it to our daily lives. I have a personal guide, and you have or can have a personal guide! Everybody's daily life is different, but that's no problem to the Almighty! He meets us right where we are and in every moment of every day.

And now here we are thousands of years later, and we can see how Christianity has expanded over the years since Jesus's death and resurrection.

Jesus told His disciples to meet Him on the mountain for His last instructions. Right before He ascended up into the sky to go to heaven, He gave them His very last words. He told His disciples what to do after He was gone. What they had to do was work! In fact, they had lots of work to do! He said for them to go and make disciples everywhere, baptizing them in the name of the Father, in the name of the Son, and in the name of the Holy Spirit.

The next thing He said was to teach them to obey all the commandments that He had given them. And He said not to worry!

Why not?

They weren't to worry because He would be with them. Yay! How long would He be with them? He said he would be with them all the way to the end (Matthew 28:16–20).

They did it! The disciples obeyed. They brought in more disciples, who brought in more disciples, who brought in more disciples until here we are today. Until Jesus comes again, this work of ours is to never end. His last instructions are our instructions as well. We are His disciples of this day and age. This mission belongs to us as well as it belonged to the original disciples of the Lord Jesus.

Jesus is coming back. Yes, He is! We do not know when this will be.

Jesus said there is not one human being on earth, and there is not one angel who knows the day or the hour when the end of the world is coming.

He said He didn't even know.

There is only one who knows this information, and He is our Father in heaven. Jesus went on to say that since we don't know, we are to stay alert and be on watch for His return!

"No one knows about that day or hour, not even the angels in heaven, nor the Son, but only the Father. Be on guard! Be alert! You do not know when that time will come" (Mark 13:32–33 NIV).

There is not one thing that any of us can do about the end of time. It started coming the minute Jesus went back to heaven! We have been in the end times ever since then. We can see the signs of its coming. It is always getting nearer. It is beyond our control. It is beyond our fretting over it. It is beyond our trying to pinpoint a date, and I do not spend any time thinking about when He is coming back. I accept the facts! He is coming back, and Jesus said no one knows when the end of time is! That's it! My main concern is to do the work I have been commissioned to do and to be on guard and stay alert, which is not an easy task! It's a full-time job! I am a soldier in God's army, and I get attacked by Satan. The enemy is always lurking around in his surveillance of me to steal me. He hates Christians. This is war. I go back into the battle again because I know I am on the right side of the battle. "I can do everything through Him who gives me strength" (Philippians 4:13 NIV).

Jesus said to just be ready. He was concerned about His work. He was leaving this earth in physical form, and His work needed to be continued, so He talked about the harvest of humans' souls. Yes, He did! He talked about the size of that harvest.

What did He say about it?

He said it was big!

And there is a problem! Oh, no!

What is the problem?

He said there are just a few workers for the big harvest (Matthew 9:37–38).

We have the same problem today as then. So how are we supposed to handle this problem? He went on to tell us the answer to the problem! He said to pray to the one in charge of the harvesting and ask Him to recruit more workers for the harvest! That is part of what we are supposed to do! Pray ... ask for more workers! Pray for more teachers, preachers, evangelists, and leaders. Pray that each Christian—men, women, boys, and girls—tells others about Jesus. Jesus will help us get the job done!

By faith, we have the kingdom of God in us. Jesus makes Himself at home in us. The Holy Spirit makes Himself at home in us. Think about that! We know what that feels like—to make ourselves at home somewhere! It's wonderful! They love living in us! They love helping us!

The job we have been given is great but not impossible because all things are possible with God (Matthew 19:26)!

Those who are willing to make the choice to acknowledge God and receive His only begotten Son can begin a journey that far exceeds anything on this earth. We become fishers of men, women, and children. We become lovers of God, lovers of life, and lovers of people. It enhances life on this earth, giving inside information on how to live it to the fullest! Life is eternal one way or the other. The choice is ours of whose side we choose to be on and with whom we want to spend eternity.

Life is good. It is wonderful! We are surrounded by family and friends. Some are here on earth, and some are with God. Even though they are with God, we are all connected.

We have freedom. God has given us complete freedom to live as we choose. And where we live is inside ourselves! We can't escape this place. It can be an exciting place, or it can be a desert that needs watering. It is the most important place of all. We can live in the world, or we can come home to our souls inside ourselves and commune with the Holy Trinity on a daily basis. It's our choice. He gives us freedom to pursue happiness and joy within. Being at peace inside is attained through each moment. Not all moments are good; each moment is different. We never know what is around the next corner, the next moment. All moments are challenging. We are so rich. We have heaven inside of us to help us live in the expectancy of the good and to work through the pain of the bad. Loving ourselves through the hard moments of life and the good moments of life, nurturing our own souls, and treating ourselves with the utmost respect keeps us at home in our own hearts. We live in the love of God; we live in the love of our own selves in a healthy Christian way; we live in the love of others. We help each other through the valleys, and we enjoy each other on the mountaintops. Jesus wants all of this for us. He calls it the abundant life. He wanted it so much He gave His life for it. He wants us to be with Him, so He is coming back to take all His followers home.

HOME

I know how my story will end! Yes, I do! The Bible tells me about it.

It doesn't matter if I die before Resurrection Day or if I am still here on earth when it happens. I am going to heaven either way!

If I die before Resurrection Day, my physical body will sleep until then, but my soul will be in the heavenly realm immediately with the Lord.

When my body dies, I will fly away to God!

"We are confident, I say, and would prefer to be away from the body and at home with the Lord" (2 Corinthians 5:8 NIV).

If I am still here when Jesus comes back, I will hear the trumpet sound and see Him coming down from heaven like lightning! "For as lightning that comes from the east is visible even in the west, so will be the coming of the Son of Man" (Matthew 24:27 NIV).

And you know what? God our Father is coming too! He will be bringing the souls of God with Jesus when Jesus comes! Doesn't that just bring tears of joy to your eyes?

> We believe that Jesus died and rose again and so we believe that God will bring with Jesus those who have fallen asleep in him. According to the Lord's own word, we tell you that we who are still alive, who are left til the coming of the Lord, will certainly not precede those who have fallen asleep. For the Lord himself will come down

from heaven, with a loud command, with the voice of the archangel and with the trumpet call of God, and the dead in Christ will rise first. After that, we who are still alive and are left will be caught up together with them in the clouds to meet the Lord in the air. And so we will be with the Lord forever. Therefore encourage each other with these words. (1 Thessalonians 4:14–18 NIV)

Oh, how exciting! The dead bodies will rise first and be united with their souls who are right there with Jesus. This will happen so fast it will be like the blink of an eye! That is super fast! Those dead bodies will be different from the old ones. They will become brand-new heavenly bodies that cannot perish. Jeremy's dead body will rise up out of that grave and unite with his soul, and he will have a brand-new heavenly body that will last him the rest of his life, which will be forever!

And then just as fast, those who are still alive shall suddenly have brand-new heavenly bodies too! They will be caught up into the clouds to meet with those who in the blink of an eye have already risen from their graves.

It makes me want to shout, lift my hands up, shout happiness and joy! Oh, hallelujah! It is exhilarating just to think about it! "Listen, I tell you a *mystery*: We will not all sleep, but we will all be changed—in a flash, in the twinkling of an eye, at the last trumpet. For the trumpet will sound, the dead will be raised imperishable, and we will be changed" (1 Corinthians 15:51 NIV).

It is a mystery!
God is mysterious!
Heaven is mysterious!
I love mysteries! Don't you?

We do not know if we will die before Jesus comes back or if we will still be living. However, it doesn't matter! It will all happen so fast whether we are already with the Lord or waiting for Him. We will all have imperishable bodies and will be ready for Judgment Day. We will stand before the great white throne of God and be judged according to the deeds we have done. Everything we have done is important to God.

It is about knowing that in the end, it is okay.

It is okay!

God knows my heart belongs to Him. Jesus knows I accept Him as my Savior, and the Holy Spirit in me is my guarantee of going to heaven. I have not been perfect in this lifetime, far from it, but I have tried, failed (sinned) many times, made many mistakes, gotten back up, and fallen down again, but I have never given up! I am still fighting the good fight; I am still keeping the good faith. I do not have all the answers. I do not understand it all completely, but that is okay too! It is beyond our human capacity to know or understand the wonders of heaven! We will be back where we belong, and we will be with God our Father!

Revelation 21:3–4 (NIV):
"And I heard a loud voice from the throne saying,
'Now the dwelling of God is with men,
And He will live with them. (This is wonderful!)
They will be his people, (This is fantastic!)
and God himself will be with them (This is powerful!)
and be their God. (This is joyful!)
He will wipe every tear from their eyes. (Thank you, God!)
There will be no more death or mourning, (Hallelujah!)
or crying (Praise His holy name!)
or pain, (What an awesome God!)
for the old order of things has passed away.'" (Everything's brand-new!)

No more tears, no more death, no more mourning, no more crying, no more pain! Hard to imagine! Wonderful to try to imagine!

Heavenly Father will smile gloriously at my arrival, holding out his outstretched arms to greet me and gather me close to him. He is my heavenly Father, my Creator, my God. He will not see my sins or punish me for any of them because His blessed Son, Jesus, took care of them at the cross. He loves me no matter what, because I love His Son.

Jeremy will be there, and with that grin of his, we will run to each other, holding each other, knowing we will never be separated again. I will always be his mother, and he will always be my son.

I will extend my arms toward Amanda, and she will welcome me into hers. She knows how I have suffered for her. Amanda and Jeremy will smile gloriously at me, and I will receive understanding of that fateful night.

I will look around at all my family and friends who got there before I did. There will be such happiness and bliss and togetherness! My heart overflows with joy right now as I think of this great reunion!

I will thank all those saints of old who are in the Bible. I want to thank them for helping me through my trials and tribulations here on earth and influencing me in my Christian life. They were human and made their own mistakes during their lifetimes on earth, but they learned from them. They never gave up the faith, and their life stories are encouraging to me. They each are unique and powerful. I love them. They are family!

Jesus will meet me as he has all of His other followers. He will look at me and beam with glory and love because on this earth I was one of His disciples. He will see me as white and pure as snow, my sins covered by His blood. This is the way He wants it. This is what He died for. He will be so happy that He will laugh out loud, and His glorious laughter will swell in me, and I will never, ever have pain again!

He will say to me, "Come with me, and I will show you the place that I have prepared for you." (Whoopee!)

We will walk and talk together, knowing each other fully! It will be a homecoming like no other, and it will have no end because ... I will be home where I belong. I will live forever, and I will be with all of you too, my precious readers who are my brothers and sisters in Christ. If I never meet you on God's green earth, I will meet you in our new home in heaven. It will be heavenly because we will know each other fully. There will never be a dull moment. The God we love and serve is mysterious. He will enjoy having His children home. It will be wonderful, fantastic, and thrilling beyond our imagination. We can't even begin to imagine it. We will meet up with the saints from the beginning of time until the end of time. Our enemies, Satan and his demons, will be gone for good. Never again will they come up against us. We will dance with joy and be surrounded by God's loving light.

Jesus wants us to be with Him. He paid the ultimate price for us and is preparing for our coming. The best is yet to come. If any of you who are reading this book have not given your lives to Jesus and you want to, then invite Him into your heart to come live with you. He is just waiting for the invitation. He loves you so much and wants to be with you and be Lord of your life. He wants you to spend eternity with Him. That is what He died for.

God bless each and every one of you in your lives down here on earth and in your work for Him. We join together in spirit; we unite together in love, and our love vapors reach up to our Father God above. He receives them with joy, and He delights in us, His children. Our big brother Jesus, who is our Savior, smiles, and the angels rejoice. We are sons and daughters of the royal family! Our presence on this earth is important, and our presence in heaven is important. Jeremy's physical presence is missed down here, but I know without a shadow of a doubt his spiritual presence is home in heaven with God our Father. Jeremy's presence is always with me in my heart until I die and go to meet him. Each and every one of us is unique in our presence. We are distinctive, individual, one of a kind. That is how God made us, and He delights in us. One day we will all be going home and be present with Him. I'll see you there.

'Til we meet,
Rhonda

Do not let your hearts be troubled.
Trust in God, trust also in me.
In my Father's house are many rooms;
If it were not so, I would have told you.
I am going there to prepare a place for you.
And if I go and prepare a place for you,
I will come back and take you to be with me
that you also may be where I am.

—John 14:1–3 (NIV)

Author's Notes

I had this book finished … or so I thought! I had a surprise waiting for me. I'll tell you what happened.

I had it edited by my precious friend Patsy B. Seay. She had been my English teacher in high school from way back when. I knew she was the one for the job. I knew she had the experience and the expertise. She worked diligently on it for as long as it took. She was wonderful, helpful, encouraging, and complimentary. She uplifted my spirit greatly. I thank her from the bottom of my heart.

I took the printed, edited pages and was correcting the mistakes in the manuscript on my laptop. I was on the last few pages of editing when my laptop died. Oh, yes, it did. I took it to Gary, the computer expert, to have it fixed, but the bad news was that it couldn't be fixed. I had worn that old laptop completely out. That wasn't all of the bad news. All the memory was gone! Oh, no! Say it's not true!

It was true.

My book was not there anymore. I couldn't believe it. There's more. The worst part was … I did not have a back up disc. I know, I know, I know … I should have known better. I did know better, but I had not done what I should have done! I had not prepared for a situation like this. Jesus said not to worry about tomorrow, but He didn't say not to prepare!

Change. Life is about change, and most of all, it is about the growth made during the changes. Spiritual growth sometimes comes with a price. That's okay. The pruning and refining are worth the pain. I sure was pruned back when I lost this book on that old laptop! I wasn't happy about it, but He gave me new growth through typing this book all over again. He knew what I needed. I was blessed during the retyping of it. In fact, when it was done, I was glad it had happened. Go figure! Only God can make something like that happen. He is mysterious! Praise His holy name!

God is my spiritual Father, and He knew what I needed even if I didn't. I was going through some more grief in my life at that time, and He knew I needed to be reminded of some things. God is so good! I love Him so. Now I probably made some mistakes in the retyping of it, so I want to thank the editors at WestBow Press for helping me with that.

I want to tell you that Jeremy's friend Joe, who was in the accident and was in intensive care for a time, came to see us after he got out of the hospital. He shared with us what he remembered about that fateful night. He said that it was an absolute miracle that he is still alive. He was thrown out of the car, and his body went through two trees. These trees were so close together that there is no earthly explanation of how his body fit through them. How do we explain such a miracle? We don't. We just shake our heads in wonderment and awe. Miracles cannot be explained. They just are, and we thank God for them. And we praise God for them. It was so good to be with Joe, to touch him, to talk to him, and to see him. We love him. I feel blessed every time I see Joe.

I had another book on that old laptop. It is gone. If the Lord wants me to write it over, I'll be with you again.

Love to all.
Rhonda

Printed in the United States
By Bookmasters